MORE PRAISE FOR
PERFORMING UNDER PRESSURE

"A criminal trial lawyer has to perform under pressure everyday. A poor performance could mean a client being wrongfully convicted and sentenced to a very long time in custody. Dr. Miller's book is loaded with useful, practical advice and interesting stories of his work with some of the world's elite performers. I highly recommend this book to anyone who performs under pressure."
  - *Brian Coleman, criminal lawyer*

"In *Performing Under Pressure* Dr. Miller provides some very practical advice on how to excel in a highly charged professional environment. I highly recommend this book to colleagues and patients."
  - *Dr. Bruce Ward DDS, President,*
  British Columbia Dental Association

"Dr. Miller truly knows the intricacies and criteria required to enable peak performance. *Performing Under Pressure* is loaded with precise and practical advice on how to excel in the moment. I highly recommend it."
  - *Rodger Schmidt, competitor and three-time Olympic and World*
  Championship Coach for USA, Italy, Austria and Germany

PERFORMING
UNDER PRESSURE

PERFORMING UNDER PRESSURE

GAINING THE MENTAL EDGE
IN BUSINESS AND SPORT

DR. SAUL L. MILLER

John Wiley & Sons Canada, Ltd.

Library and Archives Canada Cataloguing in Publication Data

Miller, Saul, 1942-
    Performing under pressure : gaining the mental edge in business
and sport / Saul L. Miller.

Includes bibliographical references and index.
ISBN 978-0-470-73764-4

    1. Success—Psychological aspects. 2. Industrial management—
Psychological aspects. 3. Sports—Psychological aspects. 4. Time
pressure. 5. Competition (Psychology). I. Title.

Production Credits
Cover design: Mike Chan
Interior text design: Adrian So
Typesetter: Adrian So
Printer: Friesens Printing Ltd.

John Wiley & Sons Canada, Ltd.
6045 Freemont Blvd.
Mississauga, Ontario
L5R 4J3

Printed in Canada

1 2 3 4 5 FP 14 13 12 11 10

To Garfield and Laara

and

to all who strive and press to excel, win, and be loved.

TABLE OF CONTENTS

ACKNOWLEDGEMENTS

I wish to acknowledge Karen Milner, Jennifer Smith, and the very capable team at John Wiley & Sons for their enthusiasm and support for this book. And many thanks to Garfield L. Miller and Laara K. Maxwell, my home team, for raising the bar with insightful feedback and editorial expertise.

I also wish to thank all of those who through our consultation, counseling, and personal interaction, or through their writings and ideas, have contributed to making the book a success: Anne-Marie, Alan, Art, Barry, Bobby, Brian, Bruce, Cam, Cathy, Carole, Charmaine, Chris, Chuck, Cindy, Clark, Cliff, Craig, Curt, Dan, Davey, David, Dawn, Deborah, Dick, Don, Donna, Doug, Fred, Gale, Gary, George, Glen, Greg, Harreson, Jack, Jenny, Jim, Joe, John, Julie, Kathleen, Kelly, Ken, Kevin, Larry, Leroy, Luke, Mark, Matt, Michael, Mitchell, Morris, Nancy, Paige, Paul, Pete, Peter, Randy, Ray, Rick, Ron, Roy, Ryan, Sam, Sean, Shaun, Sharon, Sid, Stanley, Tanya, Thelma, Tiger, Tom, Vince, Will, and Yvon. Thank you all.

WE ARE ALL PERFORMERS

For over a quarter of a century, I have been fortunate to work with elite performers—people with the talent, motivation, and desire to be the best they can be. In principle, excelling is really quite simple. It is about having a clear idea of what you want to do, acting on that idea, staying focused, and persevering until you make it happen. However, sometimes, something comes between the desire and the doing. That something is often *pressure*.

It's the sixth game of the World Series and the team at bat is trailing in the Series three games to two. It's the tenth inning and they are losing the game 5 to 3. There are two out and two runners on base. One more out and they will lose the World Series. The batter stepping up to the plate is a seasoned veteran, yet like many competitors, in his desire to excel he sometimes tries too hard, tenses up, and interferes with his performance. As he stands at the plate facing the pitcher at that critical moment in the game and the Series, he desperately wants to get a hit, to express his ability. There are 60,000 frantic fans in the stadium, 60 million more watching on television. The atmosphere is electric. The pressure is enormous.

With just one second left in the game and his team losing 29 to 27, the kicker stands poised to kick a 33-yard field goal. The field goal will mean victory. Missing the kick will mean losing the game and probably his job. It is a seemingly routine kick, the kind he made at practice over 100 times during the week. However, the previous Sunday, he missed two short field goals and was blamed in the press for his team's loss. Now he stands in front of 55,000 people, with millions more watching on national television. The game and his job hang in the balance. The pressure is enormous.

The scene is the cycling velodrome at the summer Olympics. It's the one-kilometer race, the fastest cycling speed race of them all. Three laps around the track, full speed against the clock. One chance, no repeats. The fastest time wins. The rider is only nineteen years old, the youngest in the race. Still, he has been training for years for this moment. It's what he dreams about. The whole race will take less than 65 seconds. The question is will he be able to bring it all together—his desire, talent, training, and technique? As his turn approaches, he can feel the tension building and his heart pounding. The pressure is enormous.

It's 8:48 a.m. as the young executive steps into the corporate boardroom. After several years with a large multinational company, he is about to give a presentation on the status of an account he has been managing. It's his first opportunity to impress the senior executives and CEO, and he is extremely motivated to make a favorable impression. He believes his future with the company is dependant on how he comes across in this meeting. He knows it's vital the presentation gets off to a good start. As the moment approaches he can feel anxiety and tension building. The question racing through his mind is, "Can I pull it together and really show them who I am and what I can do?"

The batter, the kicker, the Olympian, and the executive are my clients, along with many other outstanding performers. The list includes major league All-Stars, NFL quarterbacks, NHL goalies, tour golfers, and Olympians in a dozen different sports, as well as stock brokers, surgeons, writers, actors, musicians, managers, dentists, lawyers, and people in marketing, sales, movie-making, rehabilitation, and law enforcement. They all want to succeed, to win, and to realize their goals and dreams. In so doing they repeatedly face the challenge of having to perform and excel in intense, high-pressure situations. At one time or another all of them have experienced how tension, pressure, anxiety, and stress can alter their perception, undermine their confidence, affect their judgment, and limit their performance.

My job is to facilitate success, to help my clients excel. To do that, I work with both mind and body. I coach my clients to exercise more psycho-physical control, and to release tension, fear, worry, and limiting thoughts. I coach them to "use" the situation, and to tune into and focus on thoughts, images, and feelings that give them power.

In the case of the batter, the kicker, the Olympian, and the executive, I spent hours working with them, helping them to excel in just the kind of intense situations described. Our goal was that, even under extreme pressure, they could regulate their emotion, shift focus, and experience more ease, power, and impact. And they did.

The World Series batter got the game-saving hit. The next night he did it again. His home run in the seventh and final game was the decisive blow and he was voted the Series' most valuable player. The kicker made the field goal. His team won the game. In the two weeks that followed, he set a league record for the longest field goal. The Olympian rode a great race, a personal best. He recorded the fastest time of the day until the last rider surpassed it. He won an Olympic silver medal. The young executive gave a compelling and impressive presentation. He spoke with clarity and poise, and the feedback he received from the senior executives was strongly positive. Shortly thereafter, he was approached to lead a larger, more high-profile account.

The most responsive and successful of my clients share several things in common. They are motivated. They have a clear, positive idea of what they want to accomplish. They have developed the technical skills required by their sport, business, or art form. And they possess the emotional and mind-body control to integrate and implement all of the above.

Facilitating elite performers in sport and business has been a major focus of my work for over a quarter century. I see sport as a fascinating forum of human potential, a model of performance under pressure, and a metaphor for life. It's an exaggeration, a drama, and a game. Yet, in many ways, it's similar to what we all experience in our daily lives. Business is another performance area where the status quo is never good enough and there is continuous pressure to improve.

We are all performers. In the "games" we play in life, in our careers and relationships, in our challenges to excel, the pressure we experience can be very real and very intense. Like the professional athlete, our performance can be significantly limited by tension, anxiety, over-effort, negativity, and stress. A key to our productivity and pleasure is our ability to maintain a clear, winning focus and to bring more confidence, power, and ease to the moment. That's what this book is about.

Chapter 1 looks at pressure and stress. What is pressure? What causes it and how do we experience it? Two basic therapeutic approaches to dealing with pressure are outlined. In Chapter 2, we begin our discussion of high-performance programming by describing personal and professional power thoughts. In Chapter 3, we explore three different kinds of imagery (goal images, mental rehearsal, and identity images) that can enhance performance. Chapter 4 discusses the relationship of thought and feeling, and offers a prescription for achieving more psycho-physical control. In Chapter 5, we discuss the release reflex and provide a tension-release process for the entire body. Chapters 6 through 8 describe the use of conscious breathing and three breathing elements (rhythm, inspiration, and continuity) that increase feelings of power, integration, and ease. Chapter 9 introduces streaming, a way to channel energy, to relax, to enhance performance, and to promote healing. Chapter 10 describes an unusual power-balancing technique for energizing and creating equilibrium by blowing off tension. Chapter 11 explores elements of a winning high-performance attitude, including confidence, mental toughness, and a positive self-image. Chapter 12 discusses individual differences—how variations in personality and focusing style affect the ways people experience and deal with pressure. Chapter 13 discusses five elements of personal lifestyle that support both consistent high-level performance and the ability to perform under pressure.

CHAPTER ONE

PRESSURE

The mind operates at both an instinctive and a highly conscious level. The instinctive brain is an action brain. It doesn't think; it simply reacts. It serves as an energizer, transforming impulse into action, receiving incoming (sensory) messages, relaying them, and firing outgoing (motor) responses. With the conscious mind we set goals, analyze, interpret, image, affirm, reason, adjust, and respond.

When we're performing well, there's an effective and remarkably complex interplay between these two levels of mental function. However, there are times when we get frightened, nervous, and tense up, when the conscious mind overanalyzes and over-responds to incoming messages. We think too much, say negative things to ourselves, and interrupt the smooth flow of input to output. There are times when we try too hard, ignore our intuition, and worry about things going wrong, instead of focusing on being smooth and effective and fully embracing the moment. This kind of performance "dis-ease" is frequently called *pressure*.

"What is pressure? Where does it come from? Is it inside or outside you? Who creates it?"

I was seated in the office of the vice president of sales of a company I'd been consulting with for several years. The VP was interviewing for the position of regional sales director and asked me to listen in. The man being interviewed was an experienced, successful salesman. Still, it was an important career meeting for him, and he was nervous. His response to the pressure of the interview was to talk too much. He felt uncomfortable and was attempting to fill the uncertainty of the moment with sound. While trying to make a good impression, he presented himself poorly. A little conscious breathing would have enabled him to feel better about himself and allowed him to be more calm and clear. When the salesman left the office, the vice president asked me, "What do you think?"

I replied, "I think he talked too much."

"Way too much," said the vice president, "If he gets the job you'll have to do some training with him." The man never did get the job.

There are many people whose response to pressure is either to push too hard and talk too much, or to contract and withdraw from expressing their full response-ability. Either way, they are operating from the fear and pressure in their lives. Either way, the result is that they reduce their effectiveness and pleasure.

Pressure is a feeling of dis-ease that is inextricably linked with motivation and the desire to be or do something more. Pressure is about being attached to outcome, about really wanting to make something happen and feeling maybe it won't. It's about pressing to meet your goals and the expectations of others. It's also about struggling to avoid the fear, pain, disappointment, and embarrassment you associate with failure.

It's pressure that visits the golfer close to the lead when he suddenly loses his touch on the last few holes. It's pressure that gives the young pitcher the uncomfortable sensation that the plate is moving. It's pressure that robs the speaker of her confidence and ease as she stands before the audience she's about to address. And it's pressure that causes the actor to blow his or her lines in audition, the salesperson to press too hard, and the student to "go blank" in an exam.

Pressure can be intense (one young athlete competing for a place on the Olympic team confided, "If I don't make the Olympic team, I'll die.") but it is not confined to the obvious "test situation." Pressure can follow you anywhere: into career, relationships, and quiet moments by yourself. It's there when you are struggling to get ahead, and to make ends meet. It's there when you are concerned about saying and doing the right thing, and about being accepted. And it may be there at times when you reflect on the meaningfulness of your life.

The Seminar

I am standing in front of a business audience of about 200 people giving a seminar on *Performing Under Pressure*. I begin by asking the group to imagine a scene. It's the same scene I presented at the start of the book.

"It's the sixth game of the World Series. The batter stepping up to the plate is acutely aware his team is losing the game and the Series. It's the tenth inning and they're trailing 5 to 3. There are two out. It's their last chance. If he makes an out, the Series is over and his team loses." I pause for a moment. "I want you to imagine that you are the batter stepping up to the plate at that critical moment in the drama." (There's some laughter.) "There are 60,000 people in the stands, 60 million more watching you on television. You desperately want to get a hit, to come through. Imagine that you have the talent and the ability. The question is, what could you do in that high-pressure moment to help you be at your best? Even if you're not a baseball fan, please consider what you might feel like in that situation, and what you could do to perform under pressure." After a moment, I continue, "The image may seem more dramatic and high-profile than what most of us experience in our daily lives, yet in many ways it's about the very same fear and pressure. Each of us is an expert regarding pressure in our lives. Please relate some of the things that cause you to feel pressured."

My seminar audiences have some responses in common. "Deadlines": a favorite pressure stimulus.

"Just the word *dead-line* is pressure," I interject. "What does it mean? If you don't deliver the goods on time, you die? The project dies? The boss dies? Deadline is a frightening word. What else causes you pressure?" I ask.

"Being successful in my career," says a young woman.

"Quotas," volunteers another.

"What kind of quotas?" I ask.

"Having to maintain a certain sales volume," is the reply.

"Working on commission."

"Having to ship so much a day," adds someone else.

"Pressure is meeting the goals I set for myself."

"It's speaking to large groups."

"It's accountability."

"Pressure is picking up the kids on time."

"It's having call waiting."

"It's paying the mortgage."

"Making money."

Now the audience is engaged. This is about every aspect of life.

"There's pressure to be in shape."

"Being on time."

"Getting around the city in traffic is pressure."

"Being supervised can be real pressure."

"Especially if you work for more than one supervisor," adds someone else.

"It's rising production costs and trying to compete with the tide of cheap foreign imports flooding the market."

"Pressure is about trying to produce a better-quality product, for less money, in less time."

"It's trying to be a good parent."

"Staying on my diet, losing weight."

"Working for someone who's demanding and insensitive."

"Making a partnership work is pressure."

"It's trying to satisfy others."

"Pressure is playing to a four handicap."

"It's keeping up," says an older gentleman.

"Keeping up what... or with what?" I ask.

"Everything," he replies.

Laughter. The group is engaged and communicating. They are all experts. They know the subject.

"Pressure is having to make right decisions."

"It's keeping the home office satisfied, and off my back."

"It's getting the job I want."

"Getting along with the rest of the family when we're all operating on separate agendas."

"Pressure is exercising patience dressing my three-year-old daughter when I'm already half an hour late for work."

"Two jobs usually mean pressure," I remark.

"Pressure is keeping my job."

"It's getting everything done on time."

"Pressure is making the most of my life."

"It's satisfying others."

"Pressure is making enough money so I don't have to worry about money all the time."

The seminar continues. I explain, "The term pressure means to press. As you can see, all kinds of thoughts, situations, and demands press on us every day. For most people the "biggies" behind an intense desire to do well are the need to feel good about ourselves; striving to meet the expectations of others; and operating with what we believe is a limited supply of time, talent, or money.

"To summarize, pressure is a force we experience as a feeling of dis-ease, growing out of an intense desire to be or do something more, accompanied by the uncertainty and fear that we may not succeed."

What does pressure feel like? Pressure is a personal phenomenon. Many different situations can trigger it. And pressure feels
different to each of us. I ask the seminar group, "How do you
experience pressure? When you are facing a deadline with career-
altering consequences, when you feel ill-prepared, when you are
losing a sudden-death playoff game and time is running out, when
you're stuck in traffic and are already late for an important meeting, when you haven't closed a sale or got a hit in weeks, when the
bottom line is trending downwards, when the mortgage payments
look enormous, what does the pressure feel like to you?"

"It's feels terrible," says a woman in the audience. "It makes me
tense."

"Specifically where in the body do you feel the tension?" I ask.

"I feel a band of tension around my head," she replies. "I get
headaches."

"I usually feel it in my neck and shoulders," says someone else.

"I tense up and stop breathing."

"I reach for a cigarette."

"I feel it in the pit of my stomach," says another. "I can't eat."

"I eat too much."

"Pressure gives me back aches."

"When I'm under pressure, I grind my teeth."

"It makes me feel tense and irritable."

"What's the 'it' you're talking about?" I ask. "Is the pressure inside or outside you? Does something out there in the world actually
cause this feeling of tension or are you creating the sensation from

within? Until you take responsibility for creating these feelings it will be impossible to create another feeling in its place. As you can see, there's plenty of variation as to how and where we experience the dis-ease: head, neck, shoulders, jaw, bladder. And those are just the feelings of pressure we're aware of. Pressure can also be subliminal."

A client of mine had been a police officer with the L.A.P.D. for 11 years. Imagine what it would be like to work at a job where each call you respond to has a potential for explosive violence and could be the last call you'll ever make.

The policeman told me, "I didn't think that way. I used to say to myself, 'It'll be okay. There's nothing to worry about. Nothing's going to happen to me. Just take it easy and do it right.' I thought that the danger of the job didn't bother me as much as all the supervision and the internal politics. It was only after I retired from the force that I felt this tremendous weight lift off my shoulders. Almost immediately I noticed I had more energy. I slept better, related better, and drank less. For years I had been living with the pressure of operating on the edge all the time. And I hadn't even realized it was there."

Whether we are aware of it or not, what's fairly consistent is that pressure causes us to tense and prepare ourselves for fight or flight. While that may be valuable for survival in the wild, in many ways it's counterproductive for health and high-level performance in our complex, results-oriented society. In addition to the tension, the effect of prolonged or excessive pressure is that we move out of the present and begin to worry about the future ("What'll happen if... ") or the past ("I should have... "). Our sense of confidence, ease, and being in control diminishes. Our thinking shifts from a positive, creative, "I am," "I will," or "Anything's possible," to a more fearful, defensive, "Don't mess up," "Be careful," and "Just hang in there," all of which limits performance and well-being.

Some people don't see pressure as an exclusively negative force. They say they enjoy pressure and think of it as a positive creative force. Well, *some* pressure is not only enjoyable, it's essential. In physiology and medicine, pressure is a necessary part of normal function. In the sexual response, the buildup and release of pressure is an integral part of the pleasure of orgasm. In the circulatory system, it's pressure that enables the blood to circulate through the arteries and veins. What is undesirable and dangerous is to have repeated and prolonged periods of excessive pressure.

In general, people require a moderate degree of pressure to perform at their best.

Figure 1.1: Optimal Performance Range

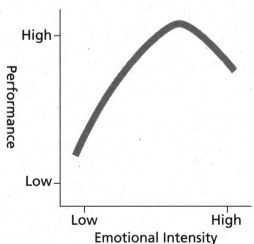

Of course, there are marked individual differences as to what constitutes optimal pressure. What is ideal for one individual may be too much for another. Relief pitchers, hockey goalies, field goal kickers, stockbrokers, air traffic controllers, surgeons, and police officers all regularly have to perform under what most of us would perceive to be tremendous pressure. Those who can perform consistently well and seem relatively less affected by this pressure either have a higher "pressure threshold," or they have developed better techniques for dealing with it.

 Pressure and stress are two terms that are often used interchangeably and they are similar in many ways. Originally, they both referred to physical forces, like air and water pressure, and the mechanical stresses operating on a structure like a bridge or building. These days they're more commonly used to describe psychological phenomena. People talk about "feeling pressure," or "being stressed." The principal difference I see is that pressure tends to be somewhat more situational and time-specific. For example, it's *pressure* that the kicker feels to make the field goal, or the golfer to sink the putt. It's the *pressure* to close the sale, finish the job on time, and "to do it right." "Stress" seems to be more general, and diffuse. We say, "It's more stressful to live in a big city." Stress is so pervasive these days it's now being used as a verb. It's not uncommon to hear someone say, "Don't stress." I don't think the distinction between pressure and stress is very important. What is significant is the pattern of pressure experienced, one's appreciation of the circumstances that create it, and learning how to reduce the pressure and enhance performance.

Feeling Less Pressured: Two Approaches

Basically, there are two psychological viewpoints about pressure and how to handle it. The more psychodynamic approach suggests that much of the pressure we experience is in part a function of the way we feel about ourselves, and that we become more vulnerable to the limiting effects of pressure when we lack confidence and self-esteem. From this perspective, it is our fear, specifically our fear of not being okay, that pressures us into feeling stressed and avoiding failure. As we become more self-accepting and comfortable with who we are, we identify less with our goals and are less in need of having to achieve and succeed in order to feel better about ourselves. *Less need means less pressure* and often better results. That's not to say we shouldn't be motivated, set goals, and direct our behavior—not at all! The psychodynamic orientation is simply that it's healthier to work from preference rather than addiction. Addiction is about responding from need. "I *need this* to happen (e.g., to get a hit, to close a sale, to be a better lover) in order *to feel good about myself.*" It's having to fulfill the need, to avoid the fear, that exaggerates the pressure. In a sense, this approach implies that if you could accept yourself more fully, you would experience less anxiety, less tension, and less inhibition, and you would be freer and better able to express yourself and realize meaningful goals.

From the psychodynamic point of view, the ideal "therapy" is one that provides insight into who you are and helps you to become more self-accepting and less fearful. It's living more as a human being instead of a human doing. Therapy focuses on insight and self-acceptance rather than on performance. It explores why: "Why are you pressing so hard?" "Why are you so concerned about impressing others?" "Why does success mean so much to you?" Therapy can be a lengthy process.

The second orientation is more behavioral. It addresses the specific behaviors involved in experiencing pressure and provides training to release tension, change feelings, refocus on thoughts and images that enhance performance and well-being, and create effective pressure-reducing routines. The ideal is to develop more psycho-physical control. That is, to have more focus, power, and ease in situations that previously were tensing and limiting. Training focuses directly on enhancing performance. It may, however, produce lasting positive changes in self-image. Treatment is usually brief.

Both types of therapy are valuable. People who lack esteem are more vulnerable to pressure. And they are more inclined to be adversely affected by it. However, from a more in-the-moment point of view, if you're about to address a business meeting, make a significant financial decision, take a test, attempt a high-pressure golf shot; if you're caught up in traffic while late for an important meeting, performing surgery, playing in a concert, or struggling to pay the bills, if you're a policeman responding to a call; if you're about to step up to the plate at that critical moment in the World Series, or attempt the game-winning field goal with one second to go and your job on the line—what you're probably looking for at that instant is not some insight into who you really are, but rather something that will give you the focus and feeling that will empower you to excel, now.

This book embraces both orientations. It explores mind-body relations, and how our thoughts, images, and attitudes affect performance. And it describes how to manage pressure-induced sensations and emotions like tension and anxiety and transform them into confidence, power, and ease.

Who Are You? What Are You About?

Who am I? and *What are my goals?* are two basic questions to consider as we enter into a discussion of the various techniques that can enhance performance and manage pressure effectively.

The Doing: I often remind my clients of two separate aspects of consciousness. One level of consciousness is what I call "the doing." I define the doer as a performer who is motivated to be the best he or she can be. The doer is goal-directed and focused primarily on what it takes to achieve his or her goals. Some of the thoughts and images (programming) that can help the doer excel under pressure are described in Chapters 3 and 4.

The Being: The second aspect of consciousness represents that part of us that appreciates that we are something more than our performance. In effect, we are human beings as well as human doings. Most of the clients I see are decidedly more in their "doing" mindset. To improve performance we address their goals, thoughts, images, and feelings. However, I believe that to excel and thrive, a balance between doing and being is the ideal. It's acquiring the

ability to be totally focused in the moment on the task at hand—
and yet appreciating that life is more than just succeeding at that
challenge.

The comments of two Olympic divers represent the extremes. The first was a young diver competing to earn a spot on
the Olympic team, who confided, "If I don't make the Olympic
team, I'll die." While that kind of thinking may motivate intense
training, it creates an underlying state of desperation and dis-ease
that can limit performance and well-being (and make living with
the aspirant an uncomfortable experience). Along with techniques
that helped the young diver excel (and make the Olympic team), I
coached her to relax and breathe. Tension-release and the breathing exercises described in Chapters 6 to 9 were very helpful. I also
counseled her to shift perspective away from a life or death mentality, to embrace the moment and the challenge, and at the same
time appreciate that life was more than being a world-class diver.

In contrast, a more balanced perspective was voiced by another
diver, Olympic gold medalist and World Diving champion Greg
Louganis, who is quoted as saying, "Even if I blow this dive, my
mother will still love me."[1] Having this broader *being perspective*
is life-enriching. Instead of performing with a survival mentality,
I encourage clients to embrace the situation with focus, power,
and ease.

---

1. Greg Louganis, sermonillustrations.com.

1

SECTION

■　■　■　■　■

WINNING PROGRAMS

A metaphor I frequently use is that the mind is like a remarkable TV set or a super biocomputer with the capability of running a diversity of programs.

If what you are tuned into, what you are thinking, doesn't empower you or give you an edge, then change the channel. Tune into positive, empowering programs.

You're the boss. It's your biocomputer.

You are in control.

Performing under pressure is learning how to run positive programs on our biocomputers. Section One (Chapters 2 and 3) is about creating and running positive programs. It discusses thoughts and images about ourselves as individuals and performers that enhance performance and make us less vulnerable to the limiting effects of pressure.

CHAPTER TWO

POWER THOUGHTS

In Chapter 1, pressure was described as a force growing out of an intense desire to be or do something more. That drive can be a two-edged sword. On the one hand, it's energizing. It moves us to action. On the other hand, the push for more creates pressure. One antidote to motivational pressure is clarity. Once a goal is defined, it is our programming that supports and sustains us in our quest to realize that goal. That is, the way we talk to ourselves, the images we bring to mind, and our attitudes can help us manage the challenges and pressure we face along the way, or lead to our disappointment.

We think 50,000 to 60,000 thousand thoughts a day—all kinds of thoughts. Thoughts continuously flow through our minds. To be a consistent high-level performer, it's imperative to think thoughts that are positive and empowering. However, research suggests for most people, approximately two-thirds of their thinking may be critical and limiting. This is especially true at times of pressure and stress. The problem is that negative, limiting thoughts create tension and stimulate anxious feelings and negative memories. Of course, it doesn't have to be that way. If what you're thinking doesn't give you power or pleasure; if you experience yourself dwelling on negatives, like, "I can't," "I doubt," "Don't blow it," or even the somewhat dubious "Well, I'll try," the solution is to take a breath and refocus on the positive. Instead of worrying and wondering, think "I am," and "I can."

Our thoughts, imagery, and attitudes comprise our mental programming. In this chapter, I discuss power thoughts—personal and professional thoughts that enhance performance. Personal thoughts are positive, self-affirming ways of thinking about who we are as individuals. Professional thoughts deal with positive aspects of the tasks that challenge us. They may include both technical and strategic elements. Creating the appropriate power thoughts and incorporating them into our lives is fundamental to both consistent high-level performance and excelling under pressure.

Matt was an intelligent young man and an excellent collegiate athlete. As a senior he was selected captain of his university hockey team. After graduation he made the challenging adjustments to become a successful professional athlete. His career went well and after a couple of years he was selected to the all-star team. Throughout the four years we worked together, one of the things I coached Matt about was his thinking. Like many intelligent people, he often attempted to deal with emotionally charged and pressure situations by over-thinking and dwelling on what could go wrong. To maximize his impact and help him perform (especially under pressure), we developed a series of power thoughts, personal as well as professional thoughts relating to game strategy and technique.

An exercise Matt did and one I have recommended to many high-level performers is to affirm, "I'm a good player," followed by four or five reasons why. In Matt's case, "I'm a good player," was followed by, "I'm smart, reliable, and physical. I am offensively skilled." And, "I'm a solid team guy, a leader." I explained to Matt that these statements defined who he was as an athlete, and were true of him regardless of the day of the week, or how well he performed in his last game. He was encouraged to repeat these statements a couple of times a day (whenever he brushed his teeth) and I reminded him that repetition builds strength.

Knowing that you are good at your job, and knowing why, builds confidence. When Matt was chosen to the all-star team, he confided, "Dr. Miller, for the past three years I've been saying I'm a very good player, but to be honest it was only when I was chosen to the all-star team that I really began to believe it." I suggested to Matt that one of the reasons that he was chosen to the all-star team was because he kept reminding himself that he was a good player—and played like it.

In addition to discussing with Matt who he was as an athlete, and to put things into a more balanced perspective, we also explored who he was as a human being. Matt understood the trap of defining himself solely in terms of how he performed, and thinking he was a better person if he played well. Matt took pride in what he did. However, he also understood and affirmed that he was a good person, a caring family member, who approached his relationships with others and the tasks he faced in life with integrity. I believe that growing a self-perspective, outside of one's job, role, or the game being played, provides balance and insulates us from the adverse effects of pressure.

In the time we worked together Matt and I also went over some professional thoughts. These thoughts relate to or describe specific actions individuals perform when they play well. I frequently ask clients to respond to the question, "When I play/perform at my best, I _____ ." I direct them to fill in the blank with a list of six to ten things they do when they are excelling, and to describe these actions so clearly that they can actually visualize them. It's excellent preparation for any challenge.

For example, Matt made this list:

- I make good breakout passes.
- I step up and support the rush.
- I get shots through from the point.
- I always have good position and good gaps.
- I play the body and finish my checks.
- One on one, I am unbeatable.
- I clear the zone.
- I control the front of the net.

I encourage clients to repeat relevant positive performance statements to themselves *before* a competition or challenge. Hockey is an intense, high-speed, in-your-face contest. I don't want my hockey clients contemplating what they should be doing during a game. I want them simply to read the situation and act. Reaffirming who you are and what you do when you are performing well builds confidence and facilitates quick recognition and effective execution. It also provides clarity and direction when perception is narrowed and thinking becomes restricted by pressure.

Jimmy was an actor who struggled with auditions. As his career developed, his interests branched out and he began to study a variety of subjects, including psychology. He reported that, with study and self-reflection, he could better interpret the role for which he was auditioning and he felt freer, less pressured, and he performed better.

As with Matt, we also explored professional thoughts. Jimmy defined himself as a good actor. When I asked him why, he replied that he was very socially aware; that he reacted to and played off other actors very effectively; and that he brought a real physicality to the parts he played—that he could adapt his body to represent the role effectively.

The mind leads and the body follows. How we think profoundly affects how we perform. Heading into pressure moments, thinking, "I'm good at this," or "I can handle it," and knowing why, builds confidence and produces results.

While consulting in Barbados, I was asked to meet with several of the country's top soccer officials. Refereeing sport at an elite level can be an intense, high-pressure experience in which half the players and much of the crowd watching may vehemently disagree with your close calls. One of the referees described officiating an international soccer match at Aztec Stadium in Mexico City, where approximately 100,000 highly emotional fans were in attendance. He said, "When I stepped out onto the pitch, the roar of the crowd literally took my breath away. I was almost frozen with anxiety. It took me several moments just to regain control of my faculties and get into the game."

I explained that having a few specific power thoughts to tune into can help cope with the feelings of pressure he described. I suggested he could prepare and protect himself with power thoughts like "I am a capable, experienced referee. I exercise good judgment." Further, I recommended he develop a few specific performance directives to tune into in moments of pressure-induced doubt or anxiety. We came up with these four: Keep moving (stay with the play); maintain a positive demeanor and posture; signal clearly and decisively; breathe.

I explained that repetition builds strength. With time and repetition, these power thoughts will gain enough strength to be useful directives that will help him be positive, in control, and effective in any future pressure challenge.

Personal thoughts can be general. They deal with power, possibility, confidence, ease, and control. They're equally applicable to sport, business, health care, and the arts—and they can extend beyond performance and doing into being. A few generic examples:

- "I'm okay."
- "I am intelligent."
- "I am response-able."

- "I'm in control."
- "I can handle it."
- "My mind is a force I use to make things happen."
- "I see opportunity everywhere."
- "I deserve to express all my ability."
- "I'm quick and strong as a cat."
- "Energy flows through me like a star."
- "I have great skill (hands, speed, eyes...)."
- "I'm patient." (The waves in the ocean never rush. And over time they can wash anything away.)
- "I'm very capable."
- "I'm a winner."
- "I'm willing to allow the success I deserve into my life."
- "I am the *master of ease*."

Sometimes a single power thought can be focusing. Early in my career, I occasionally experienced moments of doubt. When I first started working in the NFL, there were those rare moments when I wondered, "What am I doing here?" The players I was dealing with were, for the most part, bigger than I was, stronger than I was, faster than I was, and some of them were smarter than I was. At these times I found it very helpful to have a power thought or two that provided perspective and reinforced my sense of purpose. The thought I used most often was, "Just my being here makes a difference." Even in those early days I knew that I was a calming, positive influence in the war zone, and that the work we did was very beneficial for a number of players. Over time, as I repeatedly observed my work contributing to positive results, those anxious thoughts eventually disappeared.

George was vice president of operations and a super-high achiever. He was extremely successful in "making his numbers"; however, he felt he was doing it at considerable expense to himself. In the process of setting his goals for the coming year he said to me, "I thrive on being successful, and I want to continue to be as effective as I've been. However, I feel like I'm burning myself out and I want to achieve results with a great deal more ease." The affirmation we created for him was, "I am the master of ease." It was perfect. George was a hard-working fellow who was never going to take things too easily. However, the thought and image of being "the master of ease" was a balancing reminder to allow himself more time, and to bring a quality of self-respect to his work. Ultimately, it contributed to his having more impact and more joy.

In Chapter 12, I describe how different personality types respond best to different "power thoughts." Task-oriented people respond more to performance-related input referring to the specifics of a task performed—for example, "I like the way you handled _____ " (with a reference to something specific) or "You demonstrated excellent _____ " (again, referring to a specific ability). In contrast, the more feeling-oriented personality responds more to personal validation: "I appreciate you." "You're the kind of person we can count on." "You're really an important part of the team."

While most people perform better with self-talk that is supportive and reassuring, others (often extraverts) are stimulated to perform with thoughts that are challenging and sometimes critical. Whether you're coaching yourself or others, if you tend to use challenging thoughts, remember to be consistent, and don't be excessively self-critical; that only produces contraction.

Most people talk to themselves in the first person ("I'm okay; I can do it."). However, since much of what we've been conditioned to hearing has been addressed to us in the second person (e.g., "You _____ "), it may be useful to include second-person self-talk to counteract or balance what we have heard in the past.

Professional Thoughts

Whereas personal thoughts are general, professional thoughts relate more to specific tasks and techniques and focus more on the performance process. They support a performer by helping him or her address specifics that enhance the game, especially when there is a lot of pressure.

"Attack" and "smooth" are two power thoughts I frequently use to represent two states of action. In many challenges we can either address the situation aggressively, attacking it, or we can address it smoothly, with composure and grace. For example, if a downhill ski racer attacks the hill too aggressively, a wipe out could occur. In contrast, if the hill is run too smoothly, a competitive time won't be achieved. The ideal is a dynamic balance between the two extremes. And that balance is something that has to be determined by the performer as the challenge unfolds. When to attack and when to be smooth will come up in many situations in both individual and team sport as well as management and sales.

Pressure, and the anxiety it generates, can upset the ideal attack/smooth balance and can lead to excessive attack or too much "smooth." In either case, the result is a drop in performance. In counseling athletes, I often coach them to manage their level of effort and intensity, and to think *attack* when they are starting to feel too comfortable... and to think *smooth* when they are becoming overly aggressive or forcing the issue. *Attack* and *smooth* are useful watch words for pacing the performance process.

In *Why Teams Win: 9 Keys to Success in Business, Sport and Beyond,*[1] I reported on Dan, an IT specialist, who used a combination of personal and professional thoughts to build confidence, consistency, and a strong self-image in three separate roles he had with Microsoft. The diversity of his roles and the quality of his self-dialogue explain in part why Dan was an excellent team player.

These were affirmations Dan used in his software developer role:

- I am an outstanding software engineer.
- I create high-quality software and ship it on time.
- I architect my components ahead of time and refine my designs as I go.

---

1. *Why Teams Win: 9 Keys To Success in Business, Sport, and Beyond,* by Dr. Saul L. Miller, John Wiley & Sons, Toronto, Canada, 2009, Josey Bass, USA 2009.

- I create simple, elegant designs.
- I understand my customers and keep them in mind as I develop my software.
- I periodically check in with them to gather their feedback on the software I've created.
- I engage with the community that uses my software.
- I work well with other engineers, both on my team and in partner teams.
- I find defects as early in the development cycle as possible, minimizing the cost to correct them.
- I learn from my mistakes, fix those issues in other code that already exists, and avoid them in writing new code.
- I communicate my ideas well verbally and in writing. I am able to effectively explain concepts to diverse audiences, including those that have technical expertise and those who do not.
- My code is well documented and easily maintainable.

These are Dan the salesman's affirmations:

- I am an outstanding salesman.
- I understand my customers and address their needs, as well as my own and the needs of my company.
- I am ethical, honest, and forthright.
- I meet and exceed my quotas/target numbers on a regular basis.
- I proactively gather feedback from my customers and work diligently to improve my customer satisfaction metrics.

- I use my expertise and close relationship with customers to positively impact the future direction of my company's products/services.
- I cultivate business and personal relationships with my existing customers and network frequently in order to find new customers for my business.
- I represent my company in the most positive and professional manner possible.
- I exemplify my company's values.

Finally, these affirmations were for Dan the executive:

- I make rational decisions in a timely manner.
- I remove myself as a bottleneck in the process and delegate authority where it makes sense to do so.
- I balance both short-term and long-term perspectives.
- I am able to empathize with others and understand their perspectives.
- I listen to others before speaking.
- I engage at the appropriate level of detail depending on the particular topic, my own expertise, the forum, and audience.
- I communicate clearly and effectively, both verbally and in writing.
- I give strong presentations, taking my audience into account, projecting an aura of competency and confidence.

- I make others better.
- I leverage the individual strengths of members of my team and enable them to spend most of their time doing what they do best.
- I develop the members of my team, taking their career aspirations into account.
- I create a productive, collaborative team environment.
- I lead others with confidence and earned authority.
- I earn the trust of my team, my peers, and my superiors.
- I get things done effectively and efficiently.

Dan's power thoughts as a software performer, salesman, and executive are exemplary.

As an example of how to apply these ideas, here are a few performance-specific thoughts a tennis player might use: "Position ready. Racquet back, shoulder sideways." "Feet moving." "Breathe." "Read the ball" (Wilson, Penn—to improve your focus). These thoughts are especially useful in practice.

"Bounce… hit" was one performance thought described by Tim Galway in *The Inner Game of Tennis*,[2] to keep the player focused on the ball during play. Similarly, "Stay with the ball" is a thought to use between points in a match, when the mind is apt to wander to self-criticism, poor officiating, or other irrelevancies.

---

2. W. Timothy Gallwey, *The Inner Game of Tennis*, Random House, May, 1974.

When supervising (*One Minute Manager*[3] style), you might think thoughts like these:

- "Define simple goals."
- "Provide clear feedback."
- "Find something to praise."
- "Critique the behavior, not the individual."

Love is power: Indeed, it is one of the most powerful forces on the planet. Love is energizing and expansive. Another way to focus on the positive is to accentuate what we love about our process. When we love something, we move towards it with more energy, power, and enthusiasm. Some "loving" performance thoughts:

- "I love _____ ."
- "I love a challenge."
- "I love to contribute."
- "I love to sell."
- "I love what I sell."
- "I love to score."
- "I love to hit the ball."

Some of the most effective advice I could give to anyone, whether they're stepping up to the plate in a ball game, interviewing for

---

3. Kenneth Blanchard and Spencer Johnson, *One Minute Manager*, William Morrow and Company Inc., 1982

an important job, or attempting to close a sale, is bring love to the process. Instead of thinking, "I've got to _____ ," take a breath and think, "I love to _____ ." In any game, just changing the thought "I've got to," which inevitably denotes a degree of pressure, fear, and contraction, into "I love to" can provide a special feeling of ease and power, one that facilitates performance (and well-being) in any situation.

Some power thoughts work at freeing us from addictive thinking: "I don't need _____ 's approval to feel good about myself." The thought, "I don't need _____ to happen.

Mitch was a highly motivated and caring young executive in the steel industry. He was wrestling with a problem with an older employee, Gene, whom he supervised. "This guy really bugs me," Mitch remarked. "He's careless, sloppy, and slow. He's negative. He complains. He challenges everything I say. And I'm not sure of the best way to handle him."

I acknowledged Mitch for his motivation to do a good job, and we discussed a few things he could do to improve his management skills. First, I reminded him to take a breath. Bringing more ease to the moment always increases our capacity to manage a pressure situation. Then, I suggested Mitch provide a clearer structure in programming Gene's tasks and time so there was less need to interact with the man. Third, I gave Mitch a few personal power thoughts to work with, including this one: "I'm okay. I don't need Gene to be respectful of me for me to feel good about myself."

What I wanted Mitch to understand was that Gene didn't upset him; Mitch upset himself. Gene was expressing his resentment and negativity to his new, young supervisor. I explained to Mitch in so doing he was actually providing Mitch with an opportunity to become a better manager, one who could manage himself in a stressful situation. When Mitch understood that the situation with Gene was an opportunity for more self-development, he began to exercise his response-ability and to *use* Gene's negative behavior to strengthen his positive focus. At that moment his attitude shifted, the pressure lifted, and he actually began to enjoy the challenge. There's one more interesting thing to note in this example. When Gene realized that Mitch wasn't upsetting himself any more, he gradually let go of his negativity and became a more productive employee.

Create eight to ten "power thoughts," thoughts that you can rely on to enhance your performance and well-being. Create or select thoughts that nurture you, and that you will feel good about that provide balance and energy.

Think positive thoughts. The ideal "power thought" is positive, relevant, and appealing, expressed in positive language. For a skater about to hit a difficult jump, thinking and feeling "lightness," or "I'm a high-flyer" is preferable, and far more uplifting, than thinking a tensing, heavy, "Don't crash." (Tension causes contraction and makes one feel heavier, reducing lightness and lift.)

For a manager making important decisions in the face of uncertainty, thinking, "I can handle this," "I consistently make good

decisions," or, "Things will work out," is preferable and more empowering than thinking, "Don't make a mistake."

For everyone, thinking of life in terms of "opportunities" is
stimulating and performance-enhancing. In contrast, dwelling on
"problems" and "negatives" is exhausting and stressful.

Keep your thoughts functional. They can be as brief and functional as a single word, like *attack* or *smooth*. Or choose a single
affirmation that provides perspective. One journalist I counseled
traveled a great deal. He found it much easier to write in his study
at home than in hotel rooms and press areas around the globe.
Along with some training in psycho-physical control (breathing
and release), we created an affirmation he found extremely beneficial (especially when he was attempting to be creative in some
strange setting): "The world is my work place."

For several years I participated in an annual corporate goal-
setting conference. During the conference the management team
reviewed the company's performance for the previous year and created goals for the year to come. The goals were personal as well as
corporate. My job was to facilitate the managers in defining their
goals and then to work with them in creating "power thoughts" to
support them in realizing these goals. Steve, the head of product
development, was feeling the push to generate more and better
products to support the company's plans for continued growth. A
few of the power thoughts we came up with for him included "I have
a personal connection to an unlimited supply of good ideas" and "I
am at the leading edge of product innovation in America today."

Steve was not immune to criticism and frustration. One day, he was discouraged and confided, "So many good ideas get shot down here." To help him deal with the inevitable rejection surrounding him and his job, and to be more free and effective, we came up with thoughts like "I enjoy the challenge and the pressure."

- "I am a free-wheeling, spontaneous, unbounded thinker."
- "I am stimulated by the critical comments of others."
- "I am well-organized and follow through."
- "I communicate and relate well to others."
- "We're a winning team. We get the ball across the line."

When we perceive a need (whether it's to improve communication, develop a new skill, lose weight, get into better shape, or even cut the grass) and *don't* do anything about it, we often create more pressure in our lives. Using "power thoughts" can improve lifestyle issues.

On improving family relations: "There's an abundance of love and warmth for everyone in our family."

On losing weight: "I'm becoming my ideal weight." "Everything I eat turns into health and beauty."

On stopping smoking: "I *can* stop smoking." "I will look, feel, and taste things better when I do." "I enjoy breathing freely and more easily."

On exercise: "I love to work out." "I feel, work, look, and love better when I'm exercising and in shape."

Create power thoughts you enjoy. Thoughts are the food of your consciousness. Feed your mind positive, powerful, digestible thoughts—thoughts you enjoy thinking.

It's your movie. You're the director. You're the star. You're in charge.

Repeat your power thoughts often. As stated, repetition builds strength. One way to build up the body is to select a simple, effective physical exercise and do repetitions with it. One way to develop some "thought power" is to define a few clear, empowering affirmations and regularly do repetitions with them. Memorize and repeat these "power thoughts" to yourself. You can record and listen to them at various times during the day. Or you can write them down. What's important is that you develop the habit of saying something positive and facilitative to yourself when you're under pressure.

Combine your "power thoughts" with breathing and release. The limitation of many positive thought programs is that they are not psycho-physical. They don't integrate mind and body. It's difficult and limiting (if at all possible) to think positively when you are tense, angry, or depressed. It's far more effective to learn to release the dis-ease, breathe, and then focus on the positive.

Release without direction can lead to confusion and collapse. Release, breathe, and think "power thoughts." Think of "scoring goals" in whatever your performance area.

Ken was an aggressive and talented young hockey player struggling to make the Edmonton Oilers of the NHL. Shortly after he got to training camp, he developed a serious case of "making-the-team anxiety." Instead of keeping his focus on what was happening on the ice, he found himself worrying about what the coach was thinking. "Did he notice me do this? Or that? Why did he play me on that line? What's he thinking?"

Ken's desire to excel and impress was understandable. However, by focusing on the coach instead of tuning into his own competence, he was giving away his power, creating tension, which reduced his concentration and limited his play. At the end of training camp he was sent down to the minor leagues.

The following year Ken was again invited to camp. He sought me out for something that would help him to stay loose and focused. He knew that he was a better player than he had shown them the previous year and he wanted to play to his potential. (He also had some anger and some thoughts that he hadn't been treated fairly by the organization.) The program we developed encouraged him to loosen up, tune into his breathing, inspire himself, feel powerful, and think "I belong," and visualize himself playing well.

That year at camp Ken excelled. Every time he would focus on the coach and wonder, "What's he thinking?" or, "They didn't give me a chance," he'd use that limiting thought as a reminder (a stimulus) to take a breath and run a positive power thought. He would think, "I'm in control." "I've got a great goal-scoring reflex." "I'm quick and strong as a tiger." "I love to score goals." And he would imagine himself playing effectively.

The moment Ken stopped focusing on his attachment to making the team and tuned into the process of "being in the moment" and playing the game of hockey effectively, he stopped interfering with himself. He played better and had fun doing it. That year he started the season with the NHL club. Five years later he was still playing in the league.

The same pressure to impress and "make it" that Ken experienced is shared by aspirants in all high-performance fields, from sport to sales to the arts. Whatever your situation, whatever you're attempting to do, remember to breathe easy, focus on the positive, and empower yourself with winning thoughts. Think "I am..." "I can..." or "I belong..." Remember, you create your reality. You're the boss and you get more of what you think about.

TRAINING NOTES

The training suggestions at the end of each chapter are for a four-week period. They are guidelines to work with to make the most of the techniques described in this book. It's not enough to simply read and understand the principles. The only way to learn is to do. Coach yourself. Work with the techniques. Adapt them to your circumstances, to your work, to the way you relate to others.

Power Thoughts

1. Week one: Give some constructive thought to your self-talk.

- Define eight to 10 "power thoughts" (no more than 10).
- Write your "power thoughts" down.
- Memorize them. Repeat them to yourself at least two or three times a day.

Remember, repetitions build strength.

During weeks two, three, and four: review your thought list each week. Review, edit, and eliminate those thoughts that don't give you power. Add at least one new thought each week that you find stimulating and empowering. Repeat them to yourself several times a day.

2. Record your power thoughts. Listen to them throughout your day.

3. Having clear, empowering self-talk can be a source of strength and a positive focus under pressure. Remember: creative thought is one of the most powerful forces on the planet and you are the thinker.

Repetition builds strength.

CHAPTER THREE

HIGH-PERFORMANCE IMAGERY

Clear, positive intention is a quality of a winning mind. The root meaning of the word *intention* is "to stretch out." Winning intention involves stretching out or projecting a clear image of what we want to create. The high-performance mind has the ability, even under intense pressure, to tune out limitation and negativity and focus instead on power, possibility, and ease. It's an ability you can enhance with training.

Imagination is the most powerful quality of the mind. It's important to understand that the body doesn't distinguish what's real from what's imagined. It simply reacts to the mental pictures you focus on. One of the easiest ways to avoid the drag and distraction of pressure is to have a clear mental picture of what you want to do, have, or be, then tune into that image, and work to make it a reality.

We both create and react to our images. Try this simple experiment. Imagine feeling very hungry. You haven't eaten all day. Then someone hands you a plump, juicy navel orange. Imagine yourself admiring its deep orange color and the texture of its skin. You smell its aroma. As you peel the orange, its thick skin comes away easily. It's ripe and juicy. You break off a section of the fruit and pop it into your mouth. As you bite into the piece of orange, its sweet, tart, delicious juice instantly fills your mouth. Take a breath and notice that as you *imagine* the taste of the orange, you may actually start to salivate.

Almost everyone has had the experience of imagining eating something tasty, or imagining a hot, sexually arousing scene, or something frightening, and noticing a physiological response to the imagery.

Imagery is especially effective when we create multi-sensory impressions of what we want to create or achieve and then project these images into the realm of possibility. I use three kinds of imagery to help people excel under pressure:

- goal imagery
- mental rehearsal
- identity or stimulating images.

Goal Imagery

A goal image is a target set in your mind. It is a clear image of something you commit yourself to achieve. A goal image is a driver. Imagine it's a warm summer day and friends are going to the club to play a round of golf, or to the beach to relax. You, however, are going to the gym to work out. Why? Because you have a picture in mind of being on the Olympic team, and that goal image directs you to the gym and to the training necessary to realize your goal. Similarly, instead of leaving the office after closing a sale and going to the club to play golf, the account executive turns back to the phone and to making the calls necessary to achieve a target she has set for herself.

A goal image can relate to a specific achievement (e.g., winning the championship, hitting a business target, graduating from university, making the Olympic team) or realizing some personal sense of self.

When I was in college, I was fortunate to play football on a team that won a national championship. I was essentially a backup player who, because of injuries to other players, became a starter midway through the season. To improve my timing, I recall having to do some extra work with the quarterback after the team's regular practice session.

The quarterback was a major factor in our team's success. He was an outstanding all-conference player and the undisputed team leader. I admired his confidence and self-assurance. One afternoon he gave me some insight into the origins of his confident demeanor. "When I was a kid my father told me that if I wanted to be the best player on the field, I should imagine myself as the best. I should think and act like I'm the best out there, and then maybe that's what I'd become. Well, so far his advice has worked out pretty well." To this day I don't know if he imparted that bit of wisdom to shore up a rookie's confidence and encourage me to focus on the positive, or just to share something that had been meaningful for him. What I do know is successful people in many fields have described how being able to see themselves as winners helped them endure the innumerable obstacles and pressures they encountered.

I work with many talented young athletes aspiring to professional careers. I reliably coach them to hold the image of the player they are working to become five years into the future, and to train with that image in mind. It is useful advice, especially when they feel they are not progressing as smoothly as they might have anticipated.

For an athlete, one of the classic images of success is imagining yourself on the winner's platform with the gold medal around your neck, the flag being raised, and the national anthem playing.

One of the teams I consulted with had to win a gold medal in a major international competition in order to qualify for the Olympics. I consulted with them for several weeks in preparation for the tournament. We worked on a variety of techniques, including all aspects of high-performance imagery, especially mental rehearsal and the use of stimulating images. (Both are discussed later in the chapter.) Consulting with the coaching staff, we defined specific on-field performance images that each player could visualize and implement to be at their best. I created recordings for the players, highlighting specific game behavior that they could use in conjunction with mental rehearsal. Periodically, I would review with each player how his imagery sessions were progressing, and do fine-tuning when necessary.

Things went along according to plan except for one team member, named Fred. He had been a world-class player for years;

then he became ill. He was diagnosed as having a malignant brain tumor, was operated on, and then given a course of radiation treatments and chemotherapy. He was selected to the team and made a co-captain because of his past excellence over the years. And while it was unlikely that he would contribute as a player in the tournament, it was felt that his presence was a plus and that he belonged.

I treated Fred much like everyone else. However, his response was unique. Instead of focusing on the elements of mental rehearsal and the specifics of his play, Fred would visualize himself standing on the platform after the final game with the gold medal around his neck, the flag being raised, and the national anthem being played.

"That's great Fred," I'd reply, "and I want you to focus on the specifics, seeing yourself making the plays, being like a tiger, playing solid defense, winning loose balls, and setting up scoring opportunities." (Even though we are discussing goal images, like most sport psychologists, I believe that it is more productive to focus on process than on the end result.)

Fred would agree. Then a few days later, when I'd next ask him about his imagery, he would reiterate seeing himself standing on a platform, with the gold medal being placed around his neck, the flag being raised, and the national anthem being played. It went on like that right up to and even through the tournament. Fred's focus was always on the successful end result. Finally, instead of trying to get him to change channels, I simply began to appreciate his image of success. The team went on to play outstandingly well and to win the gold medal. After the final game I experienced some déjà vu. Standing in the crowd at the base of the awards platform I looked up at the team and Fred, and watched a gold medal being placed around his neck, saw the flag being raised and heard the national anthem being played.

Later, I acknowledged Fred for his belief and his clear winning focus. He made a difference. In sport and business the ability of the players to believe in and *imagine* achieving their goal is a vital part of winning team play.

On a different mission, an executive responsible for a major trade show explained to me that he not only used imagery as a blueprint of what the show should and would be, but that he'd periodically slip into the future and imagine himself after the show's successful completion. In so doing he'd see himself sitting back, feeling relaxed, having a drink at a favorite Chicago restaurant, and reflecting on a job well done. He confided that he would frequently tune into that image for sustenance and to keep his energy up during the long, tedious, and often frustrating preparatory phase of putting the show together.

Goal images both push and sustain us. Driving to the airport at five a.m., I notice a figure jogging in the dark, the rain, and the cold. I know that the jogger has a picture in her mind of something she is working towards. Her goal may be to lose weight, or to make an Olympic team. I can't tell exactly what it is by watching her run, but I know there's some motivating force behind her early morning run. It is much easier to get out of a warm bed before dawn on a dark, cold rainy day if one has a clear image of something meaningful one is working towards.

Define your goals clearly enough so that you can actually see them. Then commit to doing what's necessary to make them happen. Hold the image of the successful end result. See them putting the gold medal around your neck. Your creative imagination is boundless.

Imagery has almost unlimited application in helping people deal with any and all of the pressures of life. Pain, for example, can be a powerful, limiting pressure. While running a residential interdisciplinary treatment program for people with chronic pain, I discussed several ways people use imagery to enhance their performance and well-being. Then I asked the patients how they could adapt these images to dealing with their chronic pain.

What we focus on we magnify in our minds. If pain sufferers focus on their pain, the pain becomes magnified in their consciousness. If they focus on positive goal images, those images gain energy; and pain, though significant, becomes secondary. I observed over a six-year period that those patients who possessed a strong, clear, positive, goal image, experienced a greater increase in their sense of well-being, and did noticeably better at returning to productive, meaningful activities than those who did not

Mental Rehearsal

Mental rehearsal is a process of rehearsing in your mind the specific *behaviors* you want to manifest. If you're a golfer, mental rehearsal may involve seeing yourself hitting the perfect shot. That is: experiencing yourself with a smooth, grooved swing, head still, focusing on the ball, striking through the ball, hitting it sweet, then imaging the trajectory of the ball flying straight to the target. If other thoughts or images come to mind, take a breath, and refocus on the sensory impression of striking the perfect golf shot. Mental rehearsal can also include imagining the feeling of satisfaction that accompanies playing a good shot.

If you are doing a presentation, mental rehearsal may include visualizing yourself well-prepared, organized, composed, calmly and clearly articulating the points you want to communicate. It may also involve seeing the audience responsive and positive, and seeing yourself anticipating questions that may be asked (even challenging ones) and imagining yourself responding with clarity, confidence, and composure.

Mental rehearsal relates to performance power thoughts. I frequently ask clients to complete the following sentence: "When I play/perform at my best, I _____ ." I encourage them to list eight to ten specific actions that describe them at their best, and to describe these actions so clearly that they can actually picture themselves executing them. These thoughts can form the basis of mental rehearsal and are most effective *before* a game or event.

"Imagination is everything. It is a preview of life's coming attractions."
Albert Einstein[1]

---

1. Albert Einstein, Brainey Quote, braineyquote.com.

Use the following suggestions when mentally rehearsing your success and reducing your vulnerability to pressure and stress.

Define what you want.

Uncertainty can be stressful. One way to increase success and reduce stress is to create clear images of what you want to be, do, and achieve... and to stay tuned into these images. These images are like radar that helps a ship navigate through the fog, the dark, and in rough seas. Be specific. Write it down. Then do some constructive daydreaming. Project your energy into the images of what you want to create. As you do, your images will support you in manifesting these actions. Whenever you feel discouraged or negative, and find yourself thinking "No way," take a breath and stream energy into the images of what you want to create.

Relax—then image.

Stress reduces higher consciousness. Whenever possible, take a breath or two before putting your creative imagination to work for you. As you do, the quality of your thoughts and images will become stronger and clearer, your sense of what's possible will increase, and your ability to make these thoughts and images a physical reality will improve.

Just taking a few moments to relax and breathe will make it easier for you to imagine youself at your best. In sport that may mean being faster, smarter, stronger, jumping higher, hitting further, throwing better. In life, it's having more awareness, clarity, and patience; having a greater sense of time; communicating more effectively; having more impact. Before making a challenging sales call, take a breath and imagine being calm, confident, focused, and communicating effectively. Then make the call.

Be positive.

Human nature is fascinating. A football player can catch five passes in a game and drop one. Too often, what he'll tune into is the image of the pass he dropped, and that can be limiting. Bobby D., a veteran NFL receiver, described the pressure to me: "What's tough is not simply running a pattern and catching the ball. It's running the pattern and catching the ball after 60,000 people in the stadium, your teammates, and the coaching staff watched you drop the last one."

Being a consistent high-level performer requires mental toughness—the ability to maintain a positive image of what you want to be or do, and to stay focused on it regardless of circumstance. The only value in tuning into the negative, or what didn't work, is to determine what you can do to improve your performance. Once you're clear about that, mentally rehearse the positive.

If your marketing presentation went poorly, it's neither pleasurable nor cost-effective to keep replaying that tape in your mind and running yourself down. That simply reinforces the negative and intensifies the pressure. Instead, review your imagery carefully with a thought to improving your technique. Look at all the elements. Were you well organized? Were you informed? Were you clear about what you wanted to say? Did you hit the main points? Were you composed? Relaxed? How did you use your time? Determine what things you want to see more of (and less of) in your presentation. Then work on strengthening (or reducing) these elements. Repeatedly imagine yourself making your presentation with all the qualities and impact you want to express.

It's the same in golf. I know several PGA tour golfers who, after hitting a shot poorly, will "clear the screen." They will consciously take a breath, and imagine themselves replaying their last shot perfectly. Then they will say something positive to themselves, like, "That's who I am." In effect, they use the poor shot as a stimulus or opportunity to image and reinforce the positive before moving on to play the next shot.

Easy first.
Move from what's easy to what's challenging. Mental training, like most forms of practice, works best when you begin by imagining yourself excelling at some activity you're comfortable with, something you've already been successful at, something easy. Then move on to something more challenging.

Cindy was a junior world champion figure skater. When I introduced mental rehearsal to her she began by imagining herself performing split and double jumps—the parts of her routine she performed with ease, grace, and joy. When she could imagine herself doing that part of her program to her satisfaction she went on to mentally rehearsing excelling at four triple jumps, which were the most demanding part of her program.

To build confidence and accuracy, pro field goal kickers begin practice with short kicks and, with success, move to progressively longer kicks. Many tour golfers do the same. They start with short putts, and with success, move to longer challenges. To build confidence and competence with mental rehearsal, I recommend the same progression from easy to more challenging.

Create winning movies.

Make your imagery dynamic, like a movie (as opposed to a still photograph). Be the star in that mental movie. Script the event as you want to experience it. Then be the director. You can stop the film, speed it up, slow it down, edit it. Do whatever is necessary to imagine yourself as you want to be, whether it's being technically perfect (in slow motion), or being more patient, more powerful, more focused, more at ease... or all of the above. You are in control.

Keep it brief.

You don't have to imagine the entire performance (the whole eighteen holes). The idea is to reduce pressure and stress, not to increase it. Simply image segments (single shots) of yourself excelling under pressure. One way to keep the rehearsal alive is to keep it brief.

The marathoner doesn't have to mentally rehearse the entire two-plus hours of racing. He or she can benefit more by imagining segments or flashes, five- to 10-second highlights. What's important is to imagine yourself running with ease, lightness, rhythm, and good technique. You can run similar highlights of things you want to reinforce in mini training periods throughout the day.

Use all the senses.

Make your imagery and mental rehearsal *multi-sensory*. Most people are strongly visual and many think imagery is exclusively a visual phenomenon. Truth is, you can benefit by incorporating cues from all the senses in imagining your performance. See it, hear it, feel it and, when appropriate, smell and taste it.

The start of any competition or race is often a time when pressure has built up and is intense. One way to support yourself during this or any high-pressure challenge is to mentally rehearse a great start.

Jenny was a Team U.S.A. swimmer with good imagery skills. She came to see me at the beginning of her sophomore year at UCLA. She wanted something to enhance her performance. One of the things we worked with was multi-sensory imagery to improve her starts. To do that, Jenny would relax and breathe; then she would tune into the image of a specific competition. She would visualize the pool, the water, the floats, the scoreboard, and the competitors. She'd hear the sounds of the pool, the crowd, the public address announcements, and the echoes. She would smell the chlorine. She would feel her pre-race "nerves," tension in her shoulders, which she'd release. She would experience herself breathing in power and streaming it through her body.

Then she would change channels on her mental TV. She'd feel her feet on the blocks, like "cat's feet" with tremendous spring. She would imagine herself like a powerful, hungry lion ready to leap. Then she'd lower her gaze, narrow her focus, and shift to sound. She would tune into the voice of the starter, saying, "Swimmers, take your marks." She could anticipate the starting "bleep," hear it and feel herself springing out, "hitting the hole" perfectly, gliding through the water, starting to stretch and pull with power. After Jenny defined the elements of her starts and then began to mentally rehearse them, the pressure became more manageable and her starts improved dramatically.

Jenny came to see me again at the start of the following year. She hadn't raced in a couple of months and she was facing her first big meet of the new season against three top teams and a field that included an Olympic medalist. She volunteered that she didn't feel confident. We talked about her event, the 100-meter freestyle, and I asked, "What's the world record in that event?" She quoted some time.

"What is your goal for the season in the 100 meters?" I asked. She quoted another time.

"What is your personal best at that distance?" I enquired. Again, she mentioned a time.

Then I asked her, "What do you have to do to achieve your goal?"

"Work harder," she replied.

"That's too general," I said. "It doesn't provide us with a specific direction or image. It's important to be aware of what actually has to change in the way you swim your race for you to be at your best." There was a pause. "Check it out," I said. "Imagine the race. First, see the start. See yourself going out. Imagine the turn. Imagine the finish. Now tell me, what has to change for you to swim at a world class pace? Be specific."

Still, there was silence, so I asked, "How are your starts?"

"They're good," she replied. (As I mentioned, she had worked hard at mastering her starts the year before.)

"What about your turns?

"They're okay," she said confidently.

"And your finish?"

"I finish strong."

"Then what's got to change?" I pressed.

"It's the first 50 meters," she answered. "I go out too slow."

"Why?" I asked her.

She paused, then replied, "Because I'm afraid. I'm afraid that if I go out very fast, I won't have enough to finish strong."

"Well, that's reasonable," I said. "It's reasonable to be conservative if you're afraid of running out of gas. But to be the best in the world or the best you can be, you have to go beyond reason. You have to be *unreasonable*."

I explained to Jenny that people only tap a small percent of their resources and that most of us are capable of significant performance increments just by changing our minds. I assured her that if she went beyond what was reasonable, if she really went for it, nine times out of 10 she would have enough to finish strong.

And, if she experienced that one in 10 times when she could have performed better, then she'd know exactly what she had to work on in training to be more competitive.

"This weekend in the big meet," I said, "go out very fast. Be the first to the wall, hit a great turn, and then finish fast and strong. *Use the pressure* of the meet. Channel that extra energy and anxiety into an image of you that is unreasonably fast."

People under pressure often contract their imagination as well as their muscles. Jenny found the directive to "be unreasonable" exciting. Since we had done a considerable amount of mental training in the past, I simply asked her to do some quality mental rehearsal. Her homework assignment for the week was to spend 15 minutes a day *imagining* herself getting off to a quick, explosive start ("like a powerful, hungry lion"), going out at an unreasonably fast pace, swimming smoothly, with good technique ("stretching out, pulling all the way through, kicking with turbo legs"), hitting a great turn ("power push and glide"), and then accelerating to the finish (more "stretch, pull, turbo legs"), and closing fast ("like a shark"). The watchwords to support her imagery were "smooth, fast, technique, shark" and "unreasonable."

Several days later I saw Jenny at the meet just before the race. She seemed confident and focused. She gave me a big smile and shouted, "Unreasonable!"

In the race, Jenny got off to an excellent start. She went out very fast and was the first to the wall. She hit a good turn and had the lead. Then the Olympic medalist caught her and they sprinted stroke for stroke to the finish. The Olympian won the race by 1/100th of a second. However, Jenny was also a winner. She swam a great race, a personal best. In the second weekend of the new season she achieved her goal for the season. And she did it not by focusing on fear and limitation but by being positive, clear, and willing to experience herself as unreasonably fast.

> *All progress depends on the unreasonable man.*"
> George Bernard Shaw[2]

Jenny went on to have a wonderful year. She captained the UCLA swim team to a winning season, set a school record in the 50-meter freestyle, did well academically, and maintained an active social life. Jenny also continued to learn about the power of the mind and her ability to make things happen by projecting her energy into power images and then working to make them a reality.

Imagination is boundless. It allows us to expand possibility and it can enhance performance and well-being.

About the same time that I was working with Jenny I began consulting with three directors of a midwestern manufacturing firm. As a company they were performing poorly. Their annual sales were way down, and they were under intense pressure to produce or go out of business. I began by asking them the same

---

2. G.B. Shaw, The Quotations Page, quotations page.com, #2097.

question I had asked Jenny: "What has to change in the way you're performing for you to achieve your goals?"

Their initial response was similar to Jenny's. "We have to work harder."

"That's too vague," I replied. "I want to know specifically what has to change in the way you operate your business for you to be more profitable. Is it design, operations, marketing, or sales? What has to improve?"

"It's sales," they replied in unison.

I suggested that they knew what had to change for them to sell more effectively. "Is there a market for your product? Do you feel good about your line? Are you in tune with what people need and want? Is the territory too big or too small? Do you have a large enough sales force? Is it a matter of timing or follow up? How's your pricing? Are your profit margins adequate? Again, what has to change for you to really excel in the marketplace?"

After a moment of reflection, one of the directors replied, "I think the main problem is that we aren't aggressive enough. We don't get out, make the calls, and get the business early enough,"

"Why not?" I asked.

"Well, there are a number of things we could say," he explained. "But to be perfectly frank, I guess we just didn't believe that it would make a significant difference, and we simply weren't willing to pay the price."

"That's reasonable," I remarked. "Why rush and make an effort if the mental picture you have of the company and the market is one of limited possibility and little or no change? However, if you want to generate new possibilities and realize your potential, it's essential that you change your image of the company and your image of the marketplace."

I told them, "Success begins with motivation and a clear sensory impression of what you want to be, or to achieve. Without that vision, movement is limited. To create change, begin by defining what it is you want to accomplish or become. Then imagine yourself doing it. Imagine yourself out in the field early, optimistic, aggressive, successful, creating an unreasonable amount of interest and new business. Then work at making that image a reality."

There is a performance cycle that links our images to our thoughts and actions. This cycle shapes our behavior. Mental rehearsal is a way into the cycle. By projecting energy into our mental images we stimulate positive thought and action and can make incredible things happen.

To mentally rehearse your success, define a goal. Next, relax and breathe. Then image yourself performing well, doing what's necessary to achieve your goal. Remember, you're the director. Create images that are positive, progressive, brief, vivid, and alive. Use all the senses and see yourself really going for it.

Stimulating or Identity Images

A third way to use imagery to facilitate performance (and to decrease your vulnerability to pressure) is with images that evoke feelings or qualities you want to bring to the moment. If you want to experience power or feel more aggressive, the image of a tiger may be effective. I tell athletes, "Select an animal that would give you the qualities you want to have when you compete." Most of the animals chosen are predators who hunt without negatives and without self-judgment. Under pressure they don't worry, they simply hunt (perform). It's not by chance that one of the best golfers ever is *Tiger* Woods. An All-England soccer goalie used the image of a cat for quickness and balance. A tenacious NHL forward used the image of a tiger; another chose a wolf. An NFL fullback used the image of a bull for more explosive power. Swimmers have used images of sharks and dolphins to give them more finish and speed.

Doug was a two-time Olympic wrestler and a North American champion. However, he was frequently tense and took too much time to get going in his matches. To win at the world level, he knew he had to be more aggressive from the start. He wanted something he could focus on that would stimulate him to greater intensity and a more instant attack. He came up with the image of a pit bull. It was an animal he liked and admired for its aggressiveness and tenacity. He incorporated that image into his mental preparation. Focusing on these images not only heightens certain performance elements, it also reinforces confidence, particularly under pressure.

Of course, there are identity images other than predatory animals that one can use. One of my favorite images for people trying to make a point is that of a whip. It's late in the game. The score is tied and there are runners on base. Instead of tuning into the pressure, the pitcher looks in at the catcher for a sign and takes a breath. He feels strong and loose. He imagines his arm like a huge bullwhip. Slowly, smoothly he draws the whip back and up. Free through the shoulder he stretches it way up and out, accelerating... he snaps off an excellent pitch.

The same analogy of starting slow and smooth and then accelerating to a peak can apply in communication areas, including sales and entertainment. Whether you're pitching baseballs or concepts at a sales meeting you can use images for more ease, more impact, and more control.

If instead of intensity or power you are looking to create a greater sense of calm, patience, or ease, the image of "a rock" or "a wave" may be useful. Ron, a screenwriter and film producer, was "over-involved" in a project he had been working on for close to a decade. After several abortive attempts to make the film, it finally looked as if his "life's work" was going to be made and with a $60 million budget. Sounds great, but after years of anxiety (that he allowed to upset his health and marriage) he was so invested in the success of the film that he reacted emotionally and explosively to any idea he thought was inappropriate. Ron was a brilliant and caring individual who wanted to contribute, but his frantic behavior was counterproductive. It alienated the director and some of the actors to such an extent that they asked Ron to leave the set. To make matters worse, his dis-ease was also adversely affecting his health.

Ron said his goal was to participate in and contribute to the success of the picture. To help him communicate more effectively,

I began by showing him how to exercise some psycho-physical control. We worked with breathing and release techniques. Then I gave Ron the image of "the rock" to focus on. I told him, "You're a rock. Nothing bothers the rock. Waves can beat on the rock and it is there. You are a strong, calm, positive presence." Whenever Ron was in conference regarding the film I encouraged him to breathe easy and think, "I'm a rock. I'm unaffected by each ripple and wave. I'm a solid, positive presence. Just my being here makes a difference." He appreciated the feeling and the image. He worked with his imagery and his breathing. As he did he became more patient. He transformed his impulse to act out into an impulse to breathe in. And he imagined himself calm and unaffected, surrounded by people who were comfortable in his presence. Ron was easier to be with, and once again people began to show interest in his opinion.

Three Guidelines for Using Your Identity or Stimulating Images

Choose something with which you want to identify.

One company CEO chose an image of General Patton to spark his performance. I asked him why he chose Patton as a performance stimulus. A war history buff, he replied, "Patton was incredibly well-organized. His trademark was excellent preparation, a good game plan, speed, follow-through, and the ability to 'run them down.'" That image worked for him.

Be careful in choosing images for others. An NFL coach referred to one of his players, a wide receiver, by the name of an NBA forward that the coach admired for his scrappy, aggressive play. These were qualities that the coach wanted to strengthen in the receiver's response repertoire. The receiver, however, saw that NBA player as a clumsy hacker with no finesse. It was an image that he didn't want to identify with, so the coach's message was ineffective.

Because of the obvious parallels between sport and business, and since many corporate performers enjoy identifying with the competitive mentality of professional and world-class sport, I often use sport images to stimulate a certain bottom-line awareness.

A talented young marketing executive was in the habit of waiting for things to happen. At times it seemed like he almost expected others to do ground work before he would follow through. He was an avid basketball fan, so the company's president and I came up with the appropriate basketball imagery to define his corporate role and what was expected of him. We told him that he had been playing the game like a center, "posting up," waiting for someone else to bring up the ball and pass to him (whereupon he was effective at finishing the play). We explained that what was required of him was to play more like a "point guard"; like a quarterback on the floor. When it came to marketing, *he* was responsible for bringing up the ball, reading the situation, calling the play, and making things happen. The image of a point guard helped him understand his role. He could relate to it, he enjoyed identifying with it, and his performance fell more in line with that expectation.

Keep focal images brief.

One Ram linebacker took a moment out of practice to ask, "What can you give me that would work in a one-on-one situation, just me and the ball carrier in the open field? I want something that works in an instant. If I've got to stop and think about it, he's gone." "Think tiger," I replied. "Think of the image of a tiger with great balance and power pouncing on the runner, exploding onto his chest and driving him to the ground." He liked the image. It gave him just the feeling he was looking for.

An elementary school teacher asked what image she could use when she was feeling particularly stressed, tired, frustrated, and caught up in being the class disciplinarian.

"What is it you see as important about what you do?" I asked her.

"I think I contribute to greater possibility in their futures," she answered.

"How could you image that?" I asked.

She thought for a while, then she replied, "I give them light."

"Okay," I said, "then imagine yourself with the light of the sun inside you, and you sharing your light."

She liked the image. She felt it gave both her and the children what they needed.

To be maximally effective, a stimulating image should be something you can access simply by taking a breath and tuning into it, e.g., Patton, point guard, rock, tiger, or light.

Enrich your images with feeling.

Just as method actors are taught to use images to evoke feelings that enhance their performance, you can use images to draw on feelings to improve your performance. I suggested the image of a lion to one of the world's top shot putters. He used it in a technical way to stimulate more spring and the vertical explosiveness required to toss the 16-pound steel ball as far as any man has ever thrown it. As part of his preparation and training, I encouraged him to think, feel, and react more like a lion.

At one point in his preparation, he asked me whether or not I thought he should focus on the other competitors during competition. Meets can be lengthy, intense affairs where opponents sometimes try to "psych each other out." "Imagine you're a hungry lion," I said. "A hungry lion's focus is the prey out there and getting to them." And, since I knew him to be overly conscious of the competition, I added, "Whether a lion looks at the other lions or not doesn't really matter. What's more important is that you stay with the feeling and the focus of the powerful lion you are and then express it in putting the shot."

At another point in training we were winding down a luncheon meeting when he ordered a rich creamy dessert. "Lions don't eat that junk," I commented. "If you're serious about realizing your goals and being a lion, live like one." He looked at me, smiled, and then cancelled dessert. His involvement with the image gave him a perspective as well as the big cat explosiveness he wanted.

Imagination is boundless. Albert Einstein is quoted as saying, "Imagination is more important than knowledge. Knowledge is limited to what we know and understand while imagination encircles the world.[3]" Imagination is even more powerful than the will. To realize your imagination potential, first define exactly what it is you want to do, feel, or be. Acknowledge the creative, capable person you are. Script your performance. Then imagine yourself excelling. Mentally rehearse yourself really being there, hitting all the elements, perfectly. See yourself like a tiger, a rock, or a beacon of light. Feel yourself confident and at ease. Imagine yourself having achieved your goal.

When you experience negativity, doubt, distraction, or dis-ease, use it as a stimulus or reminder to focus on your high-performance imagery. Tune into sensory impressions of you at your best. Hold those images. Act on them. Make them real. You are the boss. You create your reality.

■   ■   ■   ■   ■

TRAINING NOTES

Winning Imagery

1. Week one: The first step towards using winning imagery is to create a clear picture of what you want to do or achieve.

---

3. Albert Einstein, Brainey Quote: braineyquote.com.

2. During weeks two, three, and four spend at least five minutes a day of mental rehearsal:

- First image yourself excelling in relaxed circumstances. Progressively increase the difficulty of the task and the pressure. It's a good practice to spend a couple of minutes at the start of each day breathing and tuning into some positive, high-performance imagery. Use the imaging guidelines described in the chapter.

- Throughout the day (during weeks three and four), run some *brief* (three- to five-second) highlights of you performing with power and ease.

- Before undertaking some important challenge, start developing the habit of taking a moment to breathe and then run a winning highlight.

- Select an identity image that feels good to you and gives you personal or performance qualities you want to manifest.

- Remember Einstein's comment, "Imagination is a preview of life's coming attractions." Imagine yourself excelling. Remind yourself: "I feel more confident and perform better when I visualize myself being successful. I create my reality."

2

SECTION

■ ■ ■ ■ ■

THE SHIFT
Positive Focus, Positive Feelings

We get more of what we think about. Having positive thoughts
and positive images leads to positive outcomes.

However, sometimes under pressure we get nervous; we tense
up and contract. We lock onto our mental TV screen the very
thoughts and images we want to avoid. We know we should be
thinking relaxing thoughts, positive thoughts, yet we're stuck with
anxious, negative thoughts. At times like that, it's important to be
able to change channels and tune into power thoughts and high-
performance images. And you can. The next two chapters describe
how to change channels and release tension.

CHAPTER FOUR

CHANGING CHANNELS

Thinking positively—especially under pressure—can be a challenge. The way the human nervous system is wired, our emotions directly affect our thinking. Unless we develop the psycho-physical control to manage our emotions, our ability to control our thoughts and images and ultimately our performance is limited.

Figure 4.1: Relationship Between Feelings/Emotions and Thoughts

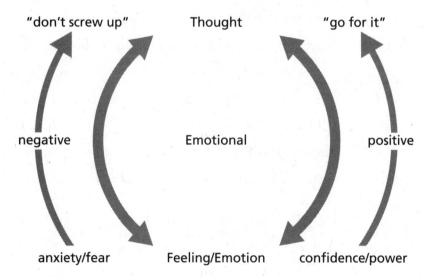

Under the pressure to perform, to be the best we can be, our emotions are often charged with anxiety—feelings of tension, nervousness, a racing heart, and shortness of breath. Anxious feelings cause tension and psycho-physical (mind-body) disintegration, which further increases feelings of pressure. Breaking the cycle involves learning to recognize those anxious feelings and being able to transform them into feelings of confidence, power, and ease. Then it's combining and supporting these emotions with power thoughts and high-performance imagery.

A favorite story of mine is about two Japanese monks. Passing through a village they were confronted by a beautiful young woman in a long silk kimono standing at the side of a muddy road. The young woman was afraid to cross for fear of getting her lovely kimono muddied. The first monk, seeing her dilemma, without hesitation walked over to her, picked her up, carried her across the muddy road, and set her down. The second monk was shocked. He stared at his companion with disbelief and anger. All morning as they continued their journey the second monk glared at the first. Late in the day they stopped for a silent meal and still the second monk stared and scowled at the first. Finally, that night as they prepared to sleep the first monk looked at the second and asked, "You look troubled, my friend; what's on your mind?"

"Sure, I'm upset!" exclaimed the second monk. "Back there in town this morning, in full view of everyone, you picked up a beautiful maiden and carried her across the street. We're monks. We're not supposed to have anything to do with beautiful young women; certainly not to carry them around in public."

The first monk listened, took a breath, then replied, "I picked her up and put her down. You've been carrying her all day."

The ability to change channels is the ability to switch from anxious, tensing, limiting thoughts or feelings to positive, empowering high-performance ones. It's an essential skill for consistent high-level performance and performing under pressure.

When I began consulting with a National Football League team, the head coach introduced me to the players. He said a few words about the importance of the mental side of the game and that I could be a helpful resource in that area. Then I got up to speak. I wanted to keep my comments brief, describe what my work was about, and have a positive effect on the group. I presented what I believe may be the clearest, fastest way to communicate the operative principle of a winning mind. What I told the team was this: "The mind is like a TV set. It watches one channel at a time and you control the switch. If you don't like the program, if what you're watching doesn't give you power, pleasure, or an edge, change channels. You control the switch." I went on to explain that my role was to assist players in developing winning programs and showing them how to change channels.

Everyone understood that tuning into winning programs would increase their possibility of success and, that they controlled the switch. The message stuck. For the next few years, whenever I was around, someone invariably made reference to the channel analogy. It was, "Doc, I'm tuned in." "I'm on the satellite dish. I can pick up anything." Following a good play I heard, "That was like an instant replay of just what I'd been visualizing." And when someone miscued, it was, "Change the channel," or, "Man, what channel are you on?"

When someone is worried about a significant pressing event, telling them to "relax" often isn't enough. It isn't that they forgot to relax. It's simply that they are locked into anxiety and don't know how to change channels. Changing channels involves being aware of negative, limiting thoughts and feelings, releasing them, taking a breath, and refocusing on something positive and productive. The act of releasing and breathing clears the screen on your mental TV. It enables you to refocus and to introduce a productive or power thought.

At spring training, there's always an enormous pressure on the young players to perform well. Of the 150 players in most minor league camps, less than 15 percent will ever make it to the big leagues. The competition and the desire to impress create considerable tension and stress. I recall working with one young player who later became a National League MVP. He was a real prospect and a tough ghetto kid who respected toughness. I remember him taking batting practice at the Mets minor league complex. He had been referred to me several days earlier because he was a talented prospect and it was thought the emotional ups and downs he experienced interfered with his performance. For example, if he made an error in the field, he might allow it to affect his next few at bats. At first he was reluctant to meet but when I explained to him our meeting was about mental toughness he agreed to participate.

We spent a couple of hours together, and I introduced him to techniques for changing channels and for focusing the mind both in the field and at bat. Now he was at the plate taking batting practice and a former major league pitcher was throwing him a lot of off-speed "junk" pitches. In his exuberance to really hit one out, the youngster was over-efforting and "squeezing" too hard. He wasn't being patient. He wasn't seeing the ball. And, he wasn't hitting it.

The pitching coach kept kidding him. The more he teased, the less the batter hit: he kept getting hotter and hotter, tighter and tighter, more and more frustrated. He seemed locked into a negative mindset. At one point, he got so angry and frustrated with his inability to hit the ball that he smashed his bat on the side of the metal batting cage.

I walked over and suggested to him that he wasn't showing mental toughness. I reminded him that he controlled the switch and to change channels, all he had to do was release... breathe... and refocus. He looked at me strangely for a moment. Then he stepped out of the batter's box and took a couple of breaths. With more composure, he stepped back up to the plate and proceeded to hit five of the next six pitches hard. When he finished batting I said to him, "That's what mental toughness is about. It's controlling the switch and controlling your mind. It's not about losing your cool, breaking the batting cage, or acting out whenever you feel frustrated or pissed off." He nodded. He went on to lead the major leagues in homeruns and runs batted in.

A key to excelling under pressure is one's ability to tune out limiting thoughts and feelings, change channels and tune into winning programs and the elements of success. To develop the ability to change channels under pressure three things are required:

1. the ability to release tension
2. conscious control of breathing, and
3. having clear positive programs to tune into.

Mike, a professional poker player noticed that as pressure built in tournaments he tended to become tense, impatient, and was plagued with anxious thoughts like, "Don't blow it."

We developed a release…breathe…refocus program for Mike with a few simple positive thoughts like, "I'm a good player." "I consistently make good decisions." And, "I love to compete." I reminded Mike that whenever he felt impatient to use it as a stimulus to take a breath and think "smooth" and "the waves never rush."

The very act of defining and setting goals produces pressure, but one of life's joys is to succeed in the face of meaningful challenges. What are your challenges? What limits you? One of the first things I do with clients is to define what it is they want to create in their lives. As we work together towards making their goals a reality, we look at the thoughts, images, and feelings that come to mind and limit them as they perform.

Fear, pain, and difficulty are three great limiters. They can sabotage our ability to perform at our best. Yet, if we prepare ourselves with meaningful goals, power thoughts, and high-performance imagery, and learn how to change channels, incredible results are possible.

For the past three decades I have worked with the Canadian cycling team in preparation for the Olympic Games. In the Team Time Trial or TTT, event, four men ride down the highway in a straight line, one closely behind another for 100 kilometers, racing against the clock. The first rider, who is facing most of the wind resistance and setting the pace, expends 25 percent more energy than the rest. After about 40 seconds to a minute in the lead he tires, then slips back to fourth; the second rider moves up to first. After 40 seconds to a minute this new leader tires and slips back to fourth, and the next rider moves to the lead. It's a grueling high-speed race across the countryside, continuously alternating the lead—with each rider pressing to maintain the pace.

In preparation for the Olympics I worked with the TTT riders for a week at the beginning of their season in early March, showing them techniques for greater ease, focus, and control. Then they went off to train and race in Texas, Britain, Belgium, Germany, and the Rockies. When I met them again in British Columbia in early July, they were in excellent shape. They were well coached and well conditioned, and they were riding very good equipment. For a sport psychologist that's ideal. You can motivate an athlete who's not in very good shape, but in a physically demanding, 100-kilo-meter race, a rider with the motivation but without the physical conditioning simply wouldn't be able to excel. However, when an athlete or any elite performer is both physically and technically prepared, getting him or her out of a limiting mindset about what they *can't* do can make a tremendous difference. That's what I set out to do in this situation. Once the Olympic team had been selected, the Olympic committee (an independent body), must approve the selection. Their job is to insure that the people sent to the games are competitive, and they won't send anyone whose performance is not up to world standards.

In the TTT, the national best-ever time then was 2 hours, 6 minutes, and 40 seconds. The Olympic committee set a standard of 2:05:30, challenging these prospective Olympians: either you take a minute and 10 seconds off the national record, or you are not going to the Olympics.

As usual, I began by showing them how to release and breathe: to feel good and to control the switch. We worked individually and in groups. As the riders became more relaxed and focused, I asked them what limiting thoughts, images, and feelings ("programs") they experienced when they raced. The three limiting "programs" they reported had to do with fear, pain, and difficulty. These three limiters apply to us all.

Fear

The fears the riders spoke about were a fear of losing control, a fear of breaking down, a fear of failure, a fear of embarrassment, a fear of letting the team down, a fear of not being okay, and the fear of crashing and injury. A moderate amount of fear can be a stimulus that mobilizes some people to action. However, in most cases, fear causes contraction, tension, limits breathing, reduces power and inhibits performance.

Pain

A second limiting program was pain. The pain experienced in cycling is a physical pain, so intense at times that a rider can't continue; some even pass out on their bicycles. The pain most of us are apt to experience in relation to performance is a psychic pain, one that threatens the ego, causes contraction, limits breathing, and, like physical pain, cuts down power.

Difficulty

The third limiting program is difficulty. Thoughts like "This is too hard," "It's impossible," or "I can't do it" also cause contraction, limit breathing, and cut down power. In each case the rider experiencing the pain and difficulty still had to continue the race—only now it was harder, like riding with the brake on.

I asked each rider to choose a single, positive thought that he could tune into whenever he experienced fear, pain, or difficulty. The thought was to be a simple, powerful one, something that was personally meaningful and that stimulated a feeling and an image that gave him power. It had to be simple and brief. The stress and fatigue of the race expresses itself like static and snow on a TV, and we wanted a stimulus word that would be comprehensible and useful under intense pressure.

Each rider selected a different word. Brian, the team's leading rider, chose the word "more." Whenever he experienced pain,
fatigue, or self-doubt he would think "more," and would go a little
deeper or a little faster. Yvon chose the word "smooth." He was
a big man who knew that under pressure he'd often tighten up
and end up having to work harder to accomplish the same result.
Chris chose the word "machine." He wanted to be inhuman and
impervious to pain, doubt, and difficulty. Whenever he noticed
himself tuning into a limiting thought or feeling, Chris would
take a breath, draw in energy, turn the wheel, and accelerate. Dave
chose the word "fast." It sparked in him the image to be lighter,
quicker, more streamlined, and aggressive. He brought that program to mind whenever he felt stressed.

The riders went out at a fast pace and stayed focused and aggressive throughout the race. Dave, Chris, and Yvon all mentioned
to me afterwards that there were times when they were hurting, and
had thoughts like, "I can't do it," "I can't keep up," or "I can't go on."
When they noticed themselves tuning into those feelings or thoughts,
they remembered to go deeper into their breathing, to change channels, to generate more power, and to refocus on their power word.
They rode the 100-kilometer distance in 1 hour, 51 minutes, and 10
seconds. *Their time was an amazing 15 minutes and 30 seconds off the
national best ever time—and an unofficial world record in that event.*

What's remarkable is that this wasn't a new team of superstars
imported from another part of the planet. Three of the four riders had been a part of the team that set the 2:06:40 mark the year

before. What was different now was that all the keys were in place. The right people had been selected, they knew what to do, and they were in good shape. And they were trained to be aggressive with their minds, to change channels in the face of limiting thoughts and feelings, and to stay tuned into winning programs, programs that gave them power.

Breakthrough experiences like this are inspiring. Sport can be a remarkable forum of human expression and a model of what people can accomplish when they integrate mind and body. This is true of both individual and team sport. And the very same principles apply to all of us, in all walks of life. When we are setting meaningful goals, developing positive programming to support our goals, and learning how to change channels and tune out tension and negativity, remarkable things are possible.

■   ■   ■   ■   ■

TRAINING NOTES

Changing Channels

1. During week one, read the book.

2. During weeks two, three, and four, whenever you experience yourself thinking anxious or negative thoughts, practice changing channels with the release... breathe... refocus formula.

3. Remind yourself: "I'm the boss. I control my thoughts and feelings. Release. . . Breathe. . . Refocus."

CHAPTER FIVE

TENSION RELEASE

One of the most common performance problems people have is that they're just too tight. In trying to excel, succeed, and win, they push and "squeeze" too much. They reduce their effectiveness and pleasure. Two of the best reasons for learning how to release tension are that it enhances performance and that it feels good. For many of my clients a practical beginning to developing greater mind-body control is learning to relax their bodies.

The word "relax" comes from the root word *laxus*, which means to be loose. To relax, then, means to regain a natural sensation of looseness and ease. The relaxation techniques described in this section are basic to high-level performance and well-being. They release blocks and inhibitions. They allow more energy to flow. And, they promote greater awareness and control.

For centuries, in some Asian cultures, all phenomena were viewed in terms of two equal and opposite forces, *yin* and *yang*. Yin is an expansive, dispersing force. Yang is a contractive, concentrating force. Neither force is better than the other. Both are necessary for optimal performance in all aspects of life. In yin/yang terms, many of the performance problems I deal with have strong yang features. That's because, under pressure, many performers tense and contract. In order to help them make balance and excel, I coach them to release.

Whenever a person perceives a dangerous or threatening stimulus, there's a natural, reflexive tendency to contract. This contractive reflex usually involves a tightening of the neck and shoulder muscles, followed instantly by a tensing of muscles throughout the body. The exact pattern is specific to each of us. It's a defensive posture that prepares us for fight or flight, and it's part of our basic survival instinct.

Many things can trigger this contractive reflex. They range from some very real external physical stimuli to some vague personal perceptions of danger. Criticism, fear of failure, and embarrassment can all trigger the contractive reflex. And it's not just what happens "out there" and what others say to us that can cause us to tighten up. The mind doesn't distinguish the source of the threat. Our own fearful, negative thinking and self-talk can also produce the contraction. Indeed, for many of my clients, the most frequent source of tension, contraction, and dis-ease is what they say to themselves.

Mind and body are one. Each thought we have is expressed in our physical bodies and in our breathing. Thoughts of confidence and competence generally promote inspiration, expansion, and feelings of power and ease. Thoughts of fear, worry, and negativity create contraction, tension, limitation, and feelings of dis-ease. If we tense up, the contractive reflex (which is part of our defensive wiring) can actually "lock in" some of the negative and limiting thoughts that we wish to avoid. The result is more pressure and more dis-ease. An effective antidote to this pressure circle is developing your "release reflex," and learning how to *use* tension as a stimulus to release and breathe.

The "release reflex" is remarkably simple; whenever you feel tension or contraction, release it... and take a breath.

Figure 5.1: The Release Reflex

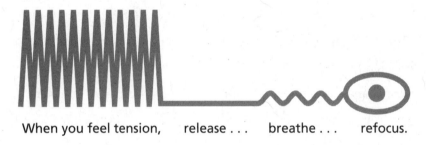

When you feel tension,   release . . .   breathe . . .   refocus.

Don't hold tension. Don't carry it around. Use any tensing or challenging situation as a stimulus to trigger release.

As he steps up to putt, the golfer experiences some tension in his hands and shoulders. He experiences himself thinking, "Don't miss this one." Then he stops. He shifts from outcome to process. He releases tension in his shoulders, takes a breath, refocuses on a good feeling in his hands, readjusts his grip and thinks, "I have great touch." He sees the ball rolling into the cup. Then he plays the shot.

The salesperson reluctantly picks up the phone. She knows the buyer she's about to call was really annoyed with their last order, which was very late. Suddenly she feels tired. She notices an uncomfortable feeling in her solar plexus. She hears herself think, "The damn production unit. It won't be my fault if the buyer doesn't write any business." When she becomes aware of what she is feeling and thinking, she stops... and releases some of the tension. As she takes a few breaths, she experiences the negativity diminish. She refocuses, and thinks, "I'm effective; I sell a fine product. And I enjoy a challenge." She smiles, then she dials the buyer's number.

When you feel tension, release it... breathe... and refocus.

Stanley was a virtuoso concert violinist. In his 40-year career he had played internationally with some of the world's finest orchestras. More recently, he had developed a specific performance problem, something he considered a "memory problem." In concert, Stanley would sometimes forget the music and "go blank." When it occurred more than once, he began to worry and wonder when it would happen again.

The phenomenon of going blank is not limited to musicians; I've seen it affect actors, students, public speakers, and quarterbacks. In Stanley's case the anxiety and embarrassment of blanking out destroyed the ease and joy he experienced playing in concert. It diminished the quality of his playing. It reduced the number of engagements he sought. And it contributed to his thinking less well of himself.

After working with Stanley and watching him play a number of times, it was clear to me that the problem wasn't his memory at all. It was his struggle in dealing with the pressure of performing in concert. Stanley was a perfectionist. He had a highly developed critical sense and was driven to "do it right." He was also a very sensitive performer who created a considerable amount of tension playing in front of a large audience, which he perceived to be critical of his performance. The combination of his desire to be perfect, his sensitivity, and his perception of the audience as sitting in judgment not only drove him to excel, it also caused him to become tense and over-aroused.

In the course of a violin concerto, with thousands of minute moves and difficult high-speed runs, it's inevitable that any performer will make a few minor slips. In his hypercritical state with his intense desire to be perfect, Stanley over-reacted to these minor glitches. Instead of flowing on when a minor error occurred, the error would trigger Stanley's contractive reflex. He would tighten up, hold his breath, slip out of the flow of the music, get lost, and "go blank."

In order to help Stanley perform with more impact and joy, we worked to develop his "release reflex" and his ability to "control the switch" on his mental TV. Our strategy was that any time Stanley noticed an error and felt himself tensing and contracting, he would release, breathe, and flow on with the music. To do that, we spent a dozen hours working with his ability to release and breathe. In addition, I encouraged Stanley to practice making errors (an exercise he didn't enjoy), then release tension and keep right on playing through them. The idea was to reorient his mindset from trying to play perfectly and anticipating an error, to focusing on playing with ease and expecting to play beautifully.

One of the more unusual techniques Stanley and I employed to strengthen his "release reflex" bears repeating. At the time I consulted with Stanley, I was living in a lovely mountain valley in southern California. My house was situated next to a cold mountain stream and about 300 yards from a natural hot spring. I spent a few hours talking with Stanley, listening to and observing him play, and showing him the breathing keys. Then I accompanied him to the hot mineral spring. As Stanley relaxed in the warm water, I reminded him to breathe easily and release any tension he was experiencing. After a few minutes of releasing and breathing, I instructed Stanley to submerge himself in the cold mountain stream. The shock of the cold stream fired his contractive reflex and took his breath away. It provided Stanley with an excellent opportunity to practice releasing and breathing. With a little practice of hot springs—cold stream, Stanley was able to release and breathe in the cold water. We repeated the cycle several times each session. Not only was it a powerful training stimulus, it was thoroughly invigorating. To further reinforce that effect at home, I recommended that Stanley practice releasing and breathing while shifting from hot to cold several times in the shower each morning.

As Stanley became more and more proficient at exercising his "release reflex," I encouraged him to integrate this ability into his hours of musical practice, particularly at those moments when he noticed himself tensing and holding. Three of the power thoughts we added to Stanley's training process were "I am in control," "I play with grace and ease," and "I play like a gypsy, not an accountant." And he did.

*Please note: While I consider the above excellent therapy

and good fun, medical and legal considerations, plus good sense, prompt me to limit recommending the experience only to those people in good health and free from any heart or circulatory problems. Please consult with your physician before undertaking a similar program.

Tension-Release

Did you ever say, "Relax," to someone who is tense? If people don't know how to do it, the advice rarely helps. One of the easiest and most effective ways to facilitate my clients is to have them do some tension-release (and then introduce the breathing keys; see Chapters 6 to 9). By tension-release, I mean having them practice tensing and then releasing specific parts of their bodies.

Tension-release is a popular treatment process. The two main reasons I use it are, first, creating tension exaggerates the feeling of release, and that's the feeling we want to highlight and reinforce. And second, tensing and releasing specific muscle groups is a focusing exercise. It will help you develop more mind-body control and enhance your ability to change channels.

Tension-release is a simple, effective way to start developing "control of the switch." To begin, guide attention to your *hands*. The hands are an area over which we have awareness and control, so they're an ideal place to begin practicing your mastery over physical tension.

- Create some tension in your hands by making fists.

- Squeeze the fists.
- Feel the tension in the center core of the fist and between the fingers.
- Hold it (four to five seconds). Release, let it go.
- After you release, take a breath.

It's that feeling of release and breathe that I recommend you experience and be able to recall.

Again, create tension... hold it... release... breathe... refocus.

Remember, what we're practicing isn't just about relaxing the hands. It's about developing your awareness and your ability to release tension. And it's about being in charge of your reactions and "changing channels."

Instead of being stressed and "at effect" of what's happening around you, *use* the situation (any contractive, limiting situation) to release and refocus.

- Once again, make fists. Feel the tension.
- Exaggerate that feeling by turning in the wrists.
- Hold it four to five seconds.
- Then, release... and breathe.

It's that feeling of release you want to experience and be able to recreate.

Next, guide your attention to your *neck and shoulders*.

The neck and shoulders area is the *primary* tension-holding area in the body. It's the number one place where people tighten up and pull back under pressure.

- Raise your shoulders up two or three inches.
- Feel the tension that creates in the neck and around the collarbones.
- Hold it (four to five seconds).
- Release... and breathe.
- Experience the feeling of letting go.

As you do, allow your head to move out and up, the spinal cord to lengthen, and the neck to be full. It's that feeling you want to recall and recreate.

One way to simulate the defensive contraction reflex is to raise your shoulders just half an inch. Experience the pressure created by such a subtle move. Hold it (four to five seconds).

Release and breathe. By voluntarily creating this response, and then releasing it and breathing, you can develop greater awareness and control of that mechanism and a greater sense of freedom and ease.

I spent several years in Europe and North America studying the Alexander Technique. The technique (named after its founder, Frederick Matthias Alexander) is a "hands on" process that teaches people to become more aware of how they *use* themselves and enables them to perform whatever they do with more ease and more effect.

What I appreciate about the Alexander Technique[1] is that it adds direction to the idea of release. The technique has two basic principles. The first is that when you experience tension, you release it and refocus. The second principle involves direction and the primacy of the head-neck relationship. Organization in the body proceeds from the top downwards; the head leads and the body follows. In practical terms it means, you release the contractive response in the head-neck area and direct and allow the head to move forward and up. The rest of the body will follow.

In trying and pressing to meet their day-to-day challenges, many people over-effort. They tense, contract, and pull themselves down. Refocusing involves letting go of this contractive response and directing or guiding the head to move forward and up; *to ease up*. Easing up in this manner enhances the response quality throughout the body.

Figure 5.2: Easing Up vs. Pulling Down

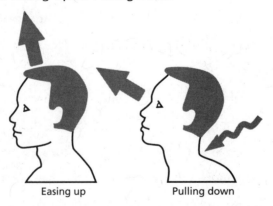

Easing up   Pulling down

---

1. Michael Gelb, *Body Learning, An Introduction to the Alexander Technique*, Henry Holt & Co., NY 1996.

- The Alexander Technique is an experiential way to facilitate both easing and performance—any kind of performance. In general, musicians, actors, and dancers have been more responsive to it than athletes and the business community. This is partly due to their sensitivity, the preoccupation with feeling and response quality in the arts, and an unwillingness that athletes and business people often have to let go of their "at any price" attitude. A basic way to support yourself and do it with less stress is by releasing, breathing, and allowing your head to ease up. Your body will follow.[2]

- The *jaws* and teeth are a part of our most primitive self-defense mechanism. Tension, anger, frustration, and aggression are all stored and expressed in the jaws. It's an important area to work with in overcoming some of our basic pressure programming. Tighten your jaws and clench your teeth. To exaggerate tension in and around the mouth, part your lips to expose your clenched teeth.

- Feel the tension clenching creates in your mouth, cheeks and jaws.

- Hold it (four to five seconds).

- Now let it go.

- Release... and breathe.

It's that feeling of letting go you want to experience and recreate.

---

2. Robert Rickover, *Without Stress: A Guide to the Alexander Technique*, Metamorphosos Press, 1988.

A genuine smile is a great release. When people smile they reflexively release the muscles in their face and jaw, plus a good deal more inside. A fake smile is another story. It's an expression of fear and dis-ease. A fake smile involves tensing many of the same muscles we contracted in tightening the jaw. Check it out:

- Create a fake smile.
- Hold it. Feel the mask of tension you are creating in your face.
- Notice you're also holding your breath.
- Now release... and breathe.

That feeling of release is the one to experience and recreate. Fake smiles are epidemic. You can see them everywhere. Whenever you spot one, use it as a stimulus or reminder for you to release and breathe. Remember, you're the boss. You deserve to feel good. And you control the switch.

Now guide attention to your *chest and abdomen*. Two of the main energy centers of the body are located in the upper chest and lower abdomen.

- Place one hand on your upper chest and one on your lower abdomen.
- Relax and breathe. Your hands are like biofeedback sensors. They're there to remind you to allow your chest and abdomen to be free to expand and contract with each breath you take. With each wave of your breath, feel your chest and abdomen rise and fall freely and rhythmically.

As you breathe, allow yourself to become a little more relaxed with each breath.

Breath is power. Tension cuts down breathing.

- Less breathing means less power... and less ease.
- With each inbreath, feel yourself drawing in energy.
- With each outbreath, allow yourself to release tension.

To "choke" means to tighten up under pressure, to cut down breathing, and to perform poorly. It's one of those popular terms that people apply to almost any performance situation.

When Carole swam butterfly, she loved to swim from the lead. When she sensed the competition closing in on her, she would contract and tighten up (especially in her shoulders). In so doing she would lose speed and power. I was asked to help her develop an alternative to contracting and "choking" under pressure. We used the tensing stimulus (in this case, her perception of people catching up to her) as a stimulus to release tension, breathe/draw in energy, and accelerate. Instead of sensing the competition closing in, contracting, and tensing, we wanted her response to that stimulus to be: breathe in energy and think, "Power, speed, ease," "free shoulders," "stretch and pull," or "shark" (as in, "I slice through the water like a shark"). To do that, we worked half a dozen times in the three weeks leading up to an important national meet. Carole learned how to put the "release reflex" to work under pressure. In her first (qualifying) heat at Nationals, she took the lead, lost it, and then, instead of tensing and "choking," Carole released, breathed deeper, refocused and came roaring back to win.

In general, people tend to perform under pressure as they have previously performed under pressure in the past. However, "choking" can be eliminated by practicing the release reflex in low-arousal (relaxed) situations until there is enough psycho-physical control and habit strength to operate the release reflex in high-pressure situations.

Practicing releasing a contractive response and refocusing in low stress circumstances increases the probability that we can and will transform tension into release in high pressure situations. If you are in the habit of tensing a certain part of your body in response to a specific stimulus or challenge, practice tension-re-lease—first in a relaxed situation, then, as you gain more control, exercise your ability to release and refocus under pressure.

A basic rule of relaxation is that tension leads to more tension… unless you use it. If you feel yourself tensing, release…breathe…refo-cus. If you experience others as tense, *use their tension* to remind you to release and breathe. I often see people with significant amounts of tension in their bodies. I don't look for it. I prefer to see ease and smiles. However, when I observe their dis-ease, I use it to re-mind myself to release my own tension and breathe. Use tension as a stimulus to create ease. Remember, if you don't use it, it will use you.

To continue the body scan guide attention to your *sexual organs*. The genitals are another primary tension-holding area. There's a muscle plexus or sphincter in the genital area that we sometimes tighten and squeeze under pressure, when we hold back in sex and in going to the toilet.

- Tighten that muscle plexus. Hold it (four to five seconds).
- Notice you've probably cut down your breathing.
- Now release... and breathe. That's the feeling you want to recall.

You can tense or release any part of your body. You can release tension in your body or your mind. You control the switch.

For men another genital-release response involves relaxing the testicles. When men are stressed under pressure (threatened), there's a contractive reflexive tendency to tighten up and withdraw the testicles—that is, to draw them up toward the body (though the actual contraction is minimal). In contrast, when men are feeling relaxed and at ease (safe), there's a subtle release of that mechanism which allows the testicles to descend more fully. In women, it may be similar in some respects to nursing mothers relaxing, releasing, and "letting down their milk."

A Question I'm Frequently Asked

While waiting for a table in a popular Los Angeles restaurant, I was introduced to the owner by my companion. My associate mentioned my work in professional sport, and the restaurateur asked for some advice on improving his golf game. "When I play golf and I'm relaxed, I play great," he said. "But, when it's important to me, like when I'm playing with friends and there's a few dollars on the hole, it becomes a matter of pride and I get tense; I rush and play terribly. What can you suggest that would help me to be calmer and play better?"

Three things came to my mind. First, I told him to breathe easy. To give himself time for the inbreath to come all the way in, and the outbreath to go all the way out. I showed him exactly what I meant. Second, I told him to calmly and clearly see the shot he wanted to make. See the trajectory of the ball flying to the target. See it land on the spot. Third, I said, "Just after you address the ball and before making the shot, relax your testicles. Allow them to release and descend as you set up, before every shot." He looked at me strangely and nodded.

I asked him, "What do you do in your work that causes you to be tense?"

"Are you kidding?" he said. "Do you know how many things can go wrong in a place like this? I'm tense here all the time."

"Okay," I replied, "whenever you notice you're tense or whenever you catch yourself thinking of something that could or did go wrong, remember what I told you to do before each golf shot. Take a breath. Give yourself time, think about what you want to create, and then relax your testicles. Not only will it help you to be more at ease and deal with things here more effectively, the continuous practice will improve your golf game."

Holding your breath or tensing a sphincter is an understandable response to pressure, but it won't improve your play. Being able to exercise greater control of subtle, intimate responses will. It's a tip I've shared with PGA tour golfers and businessmen alike.

The last tension-release exercise involves curling your toes. Make fists with your *feet*. Feel the tension in the soles of your feet and the toes. Hold it (four to five seconds). It's like a bird holding onto a perch. Performers with busy hands (e.g., jugglers, batters) and those in front of an audience (actors on stage, speakers doing a presentation) sometimes clench their feet as an expression of tension. In so doing they limit the flow of energy up through the body and lose power. Now, release and breathe. Think "cat's feet."

Feel yourself with power pads on the soles of your feet and toes. It's a feeling that will give you more spring and balance. And it's one to recall and recreate. Creating "cat's feet" is a valuable performance aid. I've used it with athletes in over a dozen different sports, but it's not limited to the athlete. The concept of "cat's feet" is for anyone who can appreciate better grounding and balance, and the power that comes from the sense of having a secure base. Release—breathe—think "cat's feet."

Tension-release is a popular relaxation technique. Our approach to the technique differs from the approaches of many other people who advocate it. For one thing, we *pair release with breathing* for a more powerful effect. What's most significant, however, is that the tension-release process we're describing is only a brief, temporary phase of the total "performing under pressure" experience. Remember, what's really important is not that you have the ability to tense or release six or seven different parts of the body, but rather that you develop greater awareness and mind-body control, and practicing tension-release makes that possible. After you've practiced the tension-release exercises about a dozen times it's no longer productive to create tension in order to create release. Thereafter, you can simply scan the body, tune in—release—breathe—and refocus. Releasing tension and taking a breath can be an instantaneous timeout that allows you to center, recharge, and refocus.

■   ■   ■   ■   ■

TRAINING NOTES

Tension Release

1. During weeks two and three, run through all the muscle groups (hands, neck, and shoulders; jaw; chest and abdomen, legs and feet) each day, tensing and releasing.

2. During week four, from time to time each day, scan the body, releasing tension as appropriate.

3. Remind yourself of a few power thoughts from Chapter 4: "I'm the boss." "I control the channel changer." "Release... Breathe... Refocus..." And a new one , "I use tension to trigger release."

3

SECTION

■   ■   ■   ■   ■

CONSCIOUS BREATHING

In Asian countries there is a cosmological appreciation that all things possess the same universal energy. It's called *chi* in China, and *ki* in Japan. The Japanese words to describe the weather, magnetism, health, sickness, and psychological states all refer to ki (weather is the ki of the sky, magnetism is the ki of a stone, health is natural ki, sickness is blocked ki, depression is dropped ki, craziness is ki that is straight but in the wrong direction.) Interesting? Perhaps. Relevant? I believe so. Especially when we consider how to incorporate or draw more of that ki into our lives. The easiest answer is with conscious breathing.

If you're like most people, when pressure builds and things get intense, you tighten up. You cut down your breathing, hold your breath, or exaggerate the exhalation. In so doing, you limit yourself and heighten feelings of anxiety and dis-ease. What's important to remember is that breathing is a powerful performance enhancer and a way out of worry overload. It's also a great balancing mechanism. You can use your breathing to psyche up,[1] calm down, improve your concentration, recharge, "get it together" and be more in the moment.

Working with clients, one of the first things I focus on is the way they breathe. It reflects the way they deal with tension and stress, and it's basic to how they feel about themselves... and how they perform. I've witnessed some remarkable performance shifts with clients who have learned to breathe with more ease and power.

Breathing is fundamental. For thousands of years people have been working with the breath for health and well-being, to raise consciousness, experience inner peace—and, more recently, to enhance performance. In the next five chapters we are going to explore breathing as an aid to both performance and well-being.

Breathing is a psycho-physical bridge that connects mind and body. So it's a great place to begin exercising greater awareness and control. Three breathing keys that I've found to be helpful in maximizing performance and well-being are rhythm, inspiration, and continuity. In the next three chapters, each of these keys is described along with examples and exercises that will help you to excel under pressure. As you read through these chapters, experiment with each of the keys. See which resonate with you and give you the feeling and performance edge you are looking for.

---

1. The words "psyche" and spirit both have as an aspect of their original meaning the word "breath".

CHAPTER 6

RHYTHM

Rhythm is one of the organizing forces of the universe. It creates order out of chaos. An effective way to regulate your emotions and to empower yourself is by tuning into the rhythm of your breath. Do you ever try too hard, especially when you really want to make something happen and notice that you're holding your breath, rushing yourself, and tensing up? That's when we slip out of our natural rhythm. We become anxious, impatient, and less effective. At such times, it's helpful to tune into the rhythm of the breath and remember, "The waves never rush."

The new Dodgers pitcher was feeling the pressure of all that was expected of him. The fact that he grew up in southern California and was finally realizing his childhood dream of playing for the Dodgers made matters even more intense. "When I'm out there, it's as if my mind is running faster than my body," he said.

To integrate the two, I suggested he tune into the rhythm of his breath. "Your breath is like waves in the ocean," I told him. "Just as the waves never rush, don't rush your breath. As you breathe, give yourself time for your inbreath to come all the way in. And give yourself time for the outbreath to go all the way out. You deserve your time."

He tuned into his breathing rhythm. He felt the inbreath come all the way in. He followed the outbreath all the way out. Almost immediately he began to feel more balanced and at ease.

I explained that the fastest way out of disintegration and dis-ease is by tuning into the rhythm of your breath. It integrates the left and right cerebral hemispheres of the brain and will enable your mind and body to perform more as one.

One week later, the same Dodgers pitcher was on the mound. He had been sent in at the start of the ninth inning to protect a one-run lead. There was one out and a runner on second base. The first month of the season had been a disaster for him. He had been charged with four losses and had an earned run average of 13.00 plus. Once again, he was in a jam.

His first pitch to the third batter was a beauty, on the outside corner of the plate. The umpire called it a ball. The pitcher could feel his blood pressure rise a few points. On the next pitch, the bat-ter hit a sharp ground ball to short, a routine out, but the shortstop misplayed the ball. Now there were runners on first and third and only one out.

The pitcher tensed. He began thinking, "Not again. Five losses in one month would be devastating. I'm supposed to be the stopper and I'm not stopping anything." The pressure of the situation, his terrible record, the bad call, and the error, all stimu-lated him to want to throw harder, too hard. More isn't always better. In pitching it's called "overthrowing" (in sales, it's "over-selling"), and it's a fear-based stress reaction that further limits performance. In the case of the pitcher, it had been a part of his poor start to the season.

Suddenly, he remembered something we had been working on all week: when you feel like you're under pressure, *breathe*. He stepped off the rubber, and picked up the resin bag. As he went through the ritual dusting, he took a few slow breaths. With each breath, he gave himself time for the inbreath to come all the way in and time for the outbreath to go all the way out. It only took a few breaths for him to regain his composure. Then feeling more focused and in command, he stepped back onto the mound, and struck out the next two batters for the save.

In the next few weeks, whenever he found himself tightening up and over-efforting, he tuned into his breathing. The simple technique of focusing on his breathing rhythm and giving himself time helped him turn his season around. He went on to win four of his next five decisions.

Another one of my clients was a "pusher." He rushed and pushed at everything he did. He talked too fast, ate too fast and, by his own admission, made love too fast. His rushing was out of control and it interfered with both his performance and pleasure in life. On one occasion I observed him at a sales meeting talking with a group of business associates. I noticed he was so intent on making his point, right then, that he stopped breathing. Characteristically he was standing there holding his breath, not really listening, poised, just waiting to jump in at the first opening of the conversation with his point of view. Seeing this, I got his attention and motioned him aside. I told him I was aware that he had something important to say. However, before saying it, I asked him to do a simple therapeutic exercise—just to breathe easily for six breaths. And with each breath to give himself time, time for the inbreath to become an outbreath. He complied and visibly relaxed. Then I asked him, "Which is the real you? Is it the guy who's rushing and stressing himself, or the man who's breathing easy and looking good?" I reminded him that he deserved his time. He looked at me for a moment, took a breath, nodded his head, and smiled.

In both the case of the pitcher and the salesman, they limited their effectiveness by trying too hard, tensing up, and slipping out of their natural rhythm.

The first breathing key is rhythm. To experience the rhythm of your breath, take six breaths. With each breath, give yourself time for the inbreath to come all the way in. Give yourself time for the outbreath to go all the way out. The key to rhythm is time.

I tell my clients that the breath is like waves in the ocean. And just as the ocean waves flow in and flow out with a characteristic rhythm, your breath has a wave-like rhythm of its own. Tune into the rhythm of your breath.

- Give yourself time for the inbreath to come all the way in.
- Allow yourself time for the outbreath to go all the way out.
- The waves never rush.
- Don't rush the breath.
- You deserve your time.

As you read through this breathing section of the book (Chapters 6 to 9) take your time. Experience what's being said in relation to your breathing pattern. Parts of these chapters are written and paced to make it easier for you to be more in touch with your breathing rhythm.

Many people have a limited or poverty consciousness. They don't believe they have enough time, talent, opportunity or money. One way to transcend that limited way of thinking is to take time to breathe. Specifically, be conscious of giving yourself time for the inbreath to come all the way in… and taking the time for the outbreath to go all the way out. Experience yourself taking your time. It is your birthright. You deserve your time.

A sense of limitation can shape our thoughts and feelings. The sense that time is limited can cause us to rush and press. Pressing leads to stress and dis-ease. Of course, the demands of life occasionally stimulate us to react quickly, and so we do. However, when rushing and pressing aren't just momentary reactions but a way of thinking and living, we slip out of balance. We become vulnerable to stress and dis-ease becoming chronic, limiting, destructive patterns. When this occurs, performance and health break down, and we "burn out." A simple, effective antidote to preventing your adaptive reactions from becoming stressful, limiting habits is to tune repeatedly into the rhythm of your breath. Remember, you deserve your time and the waves never rush. Don't rush the breath. There's power in taking your time.

As mentioned in the last chapter, shifting focus from what you are doing and slipping into the rhythm of your breath can be a momentary timeout that allows you to center, balance, and refocus.

Managing anything can be stressful. Managing a professional baseball team, like running a competitive business or caring for a large family, can mean months of almost continuous stress. In baseball, a manager has to maintain a constant vigil during the game, and decisions can be carried away from the field (office) and fill every waking hour. When you add to that the stress of dealing with enormous egos, a large aggressive press corps, and the second guessing of thousands of rabid fans, it's easy to get so immersed in it all that you forget to breathe.

Some years ago, Davey Johnson, then the manager of the New York Mets, asked me to show him something of the work I was doing with some of the players.[1] We had met several years earlier when Davey was managing at Jackson in the Texas League and I was teaching and consulting with athletes at Mississippi State University. Some of the baseball players I worked with at the time had really excelled. One tied the NCAA record for the most homeruns in a single season, and another set a conference pitching record. Being both curious and innovative, Davey was interested in what I was doing to facilitate these athletes. A meeting was arranged. It was an interesting exchange of ideas and experience. Several years later, he brought me in to work with the Mets.

---

1. See Chapter 47. Davey Johnson and Peter Golenbock, *Bats*, G.P. Putnam & Sons, NY, 1986.

Now, still curious, Davey took half an hour out from the pennant race and a seemingly endless schedule, lay back on a sofa in his office, and began to relax. With some guidance, he slipped into the rhythm of his breath. He experienced the breath as "waves" and gave himself time for the in wave (the inbreath) to become an out wave (outbreath). After just a moment or two of breathing he said, "You know, every once in awhile in the ocean there's a bigger set of waves. It feels the same with my breathing. Every once in a while, say every seventh or tenth breath, it feels like there should be a bigger breath, a bigger wave." I acknowledged his intuition. There are no rigid patterns to breathing. The keys are rhythm, inspiration, and continuity, and *what feels right to you*. And slipping into his breathing rhythm and taking the occasional big breath felt right.

Breathing is a direct path to regulating our physiology and emotions. Davey's awareness of a sense of greater ease and power was apparent. After just a few minutes of breathing, he got up with a start. "Damn!" he exclaimed. "I really haven't been breathing. Oh, I push myself to jog everyday but for me that's just more rush. This is simple enough and there's power in it. I could do with rushing less and breathing more."

Twenty years later Davey was managing Team USA in the Baseball World Classic. Watching one of his relief pitchers struggling under pressure, I noticed that the player's face was a mask of tension. I commented to Davey that the player looked very tight. Davey remarked that a lot of players like to put on a stern game face.

"A stern game face is fine," I replied, "as long as it doesn't heighten tension and suppress breathing. Breath is power."

With rare exception, the most efficient use of energy is focusing on feelings of ease, power, and flow as opposed to efforting and tensing to create a menacing appearance, in order to impress others.

Whether it's baseball or business, two things that can help a manager cope with stress are, first, seeing your employees performing well and the team being successful. And, second, having a technique for effectively reducing pressure and dis-ease. Something the Mets manager and some of his players discovered years ago was that the simple habit of tuning into their breathing gave them more patience and enabled them to see more clearly. With just a few minutes of rhythmical breathing, you can begin to reprogram yourself out of a rush and struggle mentality into feelings of greater confidence, power, and ease.

Don was director of operations of 32 shopping centers on the West Coast. His job involved keeping 1600 tenants, and the financial group he served, happy. If the power went off, if a pipe broke, a tenant closed early, if the weather was bad, if vacancies increased, operational costs went up, or sales dropped, Don heard about it. He experienced his job as continuous pressure to keep things right. What made it even more intense for Don was that he was a perfectionist who was forced to rely on hundreds of others to get the job done. Many of these others were far less motivated and less involved than he was.

Don equated his job to that of managing a baseball team of high-priced individuals, all with their own agendas and sensitivities. He described how the monthly numbers his team posted (sales volumes, operational expenditures, vacancies, and revenue per square foot) were equivalent to the numbers posted by a team of major leaguers (games won, batting averages, RBIs, earned runs). When their numbers dropped, the pressure Don felt increased. "It's easy to tell someone to 'ease up' and 'don't let things bother you.'" Don remarked. "It's another thing to actually be more at ease and still be effective." I met Don after he'd had a heart attack, and, along with recommending some significant necessary changes in his lifestyle[2], I counseled Don about his style of management.

Managing shopping centers is about managing people, time, and space. That's a challenge. To give Don the sense of having greater control, I began by working with his breathing. I explained to him, that, while he couldn't control each and every situation, when it came to how he reacted, he was the boss. In order to help him feel more in control, we focused on his breathing rhythm and his taking the time he had available to him. That is, the time for his inbreath to come all the way in…and time for his outbreath to go all the way out.

A key to psycho-physical control is pairing feelings and thoughts. As Don became more conscious of taking time to breathe, I recommended he add the thought, "I'm the boss, and the boss takes his

_____

2. The way we live day to day is important in reducing our vulnerability to pressure and stress. See Chapter 13 for input on lifestyle factors that nurture well-being and consistent high-level performance.

time." I encouraged Don to maintain this awareness at work and at play. I told him, "Whether you're talking on the phone, sitting in conference, walking the malls, or reviewing numbers, you can always take the time to breathe consciously. Similarly, when you're exercising, eating, being social, or playing golf, be conscious of experiencing your time: time for the inbreath to come all the way in and the outbreath go all the way out. The boss takes his time."

Like many high achievers, Don was concerned that if he eased up, his performance would go down. What he discovered was that taking time to breathe allowed him to perform or operate at a healthier and *more* productive pace. He was aware that his earlier style of rushing and pushing himself had contributed to his heart attack and he was pleased with the change. Referring to his ability to stay tuned into the rhythm of his breath, Don joked, "It's the ultimate pacemaker."

The first breathing key to performing under pressure is rhythm.

Rhythm is about using your time. It's allowing yourself time for the breath to change directions. Remember, you're the boss and the boss takes his or her time.

- Again, experience your breathing rhythm. Take six breaths.
- Give yourself time for the inbreath to come all the way in.
- Allow yourself time for the outbreath to go all the way out.
- Don't rush the breath.
- Don't force it or try to control it; experience the rhythm of your breathing.

- After a few breaths pick up the point where the breath changes direction—where the inbreath becomes an outbreath, or the outbreath becomes an inbreath. That is a power point.

Figure 6.1: The Power Point

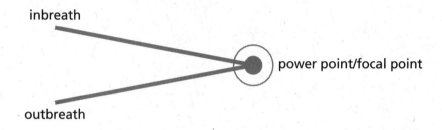

The mind may wander, but one way to stay focused on your breathing rhythm and to stay in the moment is to pick up that point. It is a focal point.

- Relax and experience the rhythm of your breath.
- There's power in rhythm.
- The waves never rush.
- You deserve your time.

A few technical suggestions on breathing: It's almost always preferable to breathe through your nose. Energy is more easily and efficiently processed breathing through the nose than through the mouth. Allow both your chest and abdomen to be free to expand and contract as you breathe. Placing one hand on the chest and one on the abdomen increases awareness and feeling. And keep it simple. (Don't worry about whether your abdomen should expand before your chest, or your chest before your abdomen.)

Breathing with ease and power is not about taking large breaths. Once you've tuned into the three "keys," you can increase (or decrease) the amplitude or size of your breath according to the circumstances and the way you feel.

■   ■   ■   ■   ■

TRAINING NOTES

Rhythmical Breathing

Take a five- to ten-minute "conscious breathing session" every day. As you do, tune into your breathing rhythm. Follow your inbreath all the way in until it starts to go out. Follow your outbreath all the way out until it starts to come in. Experience the rhythm of your breath.

- During week one: At least two or three times a day, consciously take *six connected breaths*. Pick up your breathing rhythm. With each breath, give yourself time for the inbreath to come all the way in. Give yourself time for the outbreath to go all the way out... and think, "There is time enough for me," and "The waves never rush."

You can also give yourself more psychological space, which will enhance your perception and your reactions to people and events around you, simply by remembering to breathe and thinking, "I'm the boss," and "The boss takes time to breathe."

I like to combine a feeling (the feeling of breathing rhythm) with a thought. Thoughts you can think anytime, whether you are with a client, in a meeting, or on the first tee include "There's power in rhythm," "The waves never rush," and "I deserve my time." It's advice I've shared with many of the planet's elite performers.

CHAPTER 7

INSPIRATION

"If breathing is respiration, then the inbreath is the inspiration."

From time to time almost everyone experiences some self-doubt. Under pressure some people think the worst. They think, "I can't," or "There's no way." They operate as if there just isn't enough for them; not enough time, opportunity, luck, or love. Truth is, each of us has a personal connection to an unlimited supply of energy, power, and good ideas. A simple, effective way to tap your power supply and to *inspire* yourself is to focus on breathing *in* energy and thinking of things being possible.

Thoughts can be inspiring. They gain maximum strength and impact in a context that nurtures them. One way to create that context is to focus on drawing *in* energy with each breath. Each breath is really an opportunity to reaffirm your aliveness and response-ability. You can inspire yourself with each breath you take.

- The second breathing key is inspiration.
- Inspiration literally means to take in spirit (or life energy).

- In this context it means to focus on the inbreath—on breathing in energy.
- Each one of us is surrounded by a limitless sea of energy.
- With each breath we can draw on that energy and draw in power.
- With each breath we can reaffirm our aliveness and direction.
- With each breath we can inspire ourselves.

Being a goalie in the National Hockey League may be the most high-pressure, intense job in all of pro sport. You are the last line of defense and your mistakes are glaringly obvious. Jacques Plante, a legendary NHL goalie, once said, "Imagine a job where every time you make a mistake a red light goes on and 15,000 people stand up and cheer. That's pressure."[1]

Glen was an All-Star, a fifteen-year veteran goalie in the National Hockey League. Going into the Stanley Cup playoffs he wanted some input, something that might give him an edge; he gave me a call. We had worked together for years so I just reminded him of what we had focused on in the past: staying in the moment, experiencing one breath at a time, one shot at a time, one period at a time, and seeing himself making the plays (his ABCs), playing his angles, stopping shots, controlling rebounds, and being "like a cat." In essence, I reminded him of the basics: conscious breathing, focusing on the positive, and being a capable performer.

---

1. Jacques Plante quote: Dr. Saul L. Miller, *Hockey Tough: Winning the Mental Game*, Human Kinetics, Champaign, IL, 2003.

Glen split playing the first two series of the playoffs with the team's other goalie. Then his colleague was benched. With his team on the brink of elimination (down three games to one in the best-of-seven series), Glen was called upon to make a difference and he played great. He recorded the team's first playoff shutout in 21 years. Two nights later he did it again. His team went on to win the divisional championship.

When I spoke to him about his performance the day after his first shutout, he said, "With about ten minutes to go in the game, I started to experience some real doubt. I recall thinking, 'Something's going to happen: this is too good to last.' Then I noticed what I was thinking, so I took a breath, inspired myself, and refocused on the positive. I thought of being 'like a cat,' playing the angles, being quick, and staying in the moment. After that, I *knew* I could stop anything." A moment later he made another big save to preserve the shutout.

A more subtle, pervasive stress is the one we all face as players in a consumer society. Many of us are bothered by repeated unsolicited phone calls, at home, and often in evening hours, from salespeople offering "an opportunity" to buy something, or invest in some "high-yield," low-risk program that sounds like it can't miss. It's part of a constant background of noise and pressure that intrudes on us to buy more, be more, and do more. After a number of these calls, it's not surprising that we often react to the next caller with little patience, unless we learn to use the disruption as a stimulus to draw in energy.

What you are less apt to consider unless you've had some experience with cold calling is that on the other end of the phone the young broker receives her twenty-seventh straight "No, thank you" response. Instead of losing power and thinking, "What's the use," or "I'm ineffective" (the kind of negativity that contributes to an over 50 percent attrition rate amongst stock brokers within their first year in the business), she uses the rejection as a stimulus to take a breath. She consciously *draws in energy*, inspires herself, refocuses on the positive, then moves on to the next call.

Many people don't exercise that response-ability. They look to something or someone else for inspiration. Their breathing becomes more shallow and limited. Tension builds, and they release it with the proverbial sigh of relief. Then, they go back to more limited breathing and the cycle repeats itself. The problem with limited breathing is that it's low-energy. Instead, focus on the inbreath. Focus on consciously drawing in power, on inspiring yourself and taking charge. Then allow yourself to release and exhale.

Something I've noticed again and again is that when people are performing well they appear confident and relaxed. They breathe easily and naturally, and they don't think about their process. However, when they're struggling or in a slump, they tense up, cut down their breathing, worry, and interfere with themselves. Shifting from a low- to a high-performance mindset becomes much easier when people remember to breathe and inspire themselves.

A World Series Wonder

After a series of ailments and injuries, Ray found himself struggling at the plate. As a former major league All-Star, his lack of
success caused him both frustration and embarrassment. He began to tighten up and interfere with his breathing, which made
it harder for him to see and react quickly to the ball. I did some
work with Ray on his breathing. First we focused on rhythm; on
his taking his time, then on inspiration, on breathing *in* power.
Ray picked up these two keys immediately. Then we added some
high-performance imagery and power thoughts. (As I said earlier,
breath and thought go together. They are the fundamentals of human consciousness.) Next, we worked at bringing this process to
the "on deck" circle and to enhancing Ray's experience at the plate.
The intention was for Ray to inspire and empower himself with his
breathing and some power thinking before stepping to the plate.

Learning is often a gradual process. Several weeks after our first
sessions, I was sitting at home watching Ray play on TV and noticed
he was again tensing and pressing at the plate. Instead of breathing
easily, he was holding his breath, then pushing out the exhalation—a
sign of pressure. Not surprisingly, Ray wasn't hitting the ball well. I
spoke with him at his hotel the following day and asked how things
were going. He replied that for the past few days he hadn't been at
all comfortable at the plate. "Are you feeling impatient?" I asked.

"Exactly," he replied. "I'm not waiting for my pitch. I'm jumping at the ball." Then he paused and asked, "What made you say
impatient?"

I explained what I observed was that he wasn't taking time to breathe, and that he was forcing the outbreath. I told him that, in my experience, pushing or forcing the outbreath was often a sign of nervousness and impatience. I reminded Ray that he was the boss, that he knew what to do to take charge; namely, tune into his breathing, draw in energy, and instead of thinking, "I've got to get a hit," affirm, "I love to hit the ball."

Fourteen months and half a dozen sessions later, Ray was playing in the World Series. Following an outstanding season, during which he had been one of the league's top 10 hitters, he began to struggle. In the Championship Series he hit in the .160s (an ineffective batting average that meant he got 1.6 hits in every 10 at-bats). And he was hitless after game two of the World Series. Whether it was the pressure of post-season play, his intense desire to excel, great pitching, or all three, Ray was again rushing himself, squeezing too hard, and playing uninspired baseball.

I called him at his hotel room on the road the morning of game three. He acknowledged his frustration and impatience. I reminded him of something simple and powerful, something we'd spent hours working on, and something that would help him be more calm and focused in front of 40,000-plus screaming fans in the ballpark that night: I reminded him to breathe; specifically, to take his time and focus on drawing energy to him. With all the stimuli competing for his attention, his breathing would give him more patience. It would help him to relax, see the ball better, and not jump at it. Following the call, his performance improved dramatically.

He got a couple of hits that night and he went on to hit .500 for the rest of the series.

In this book's introduction, I described Ray coming to the plate in that critical situation in the sixth game of the World Series. There were two out, two men on base, and his team was losing by two runs. One more out and they'd lose the World Series. As Ray stepped up to the plate, he consciously focused on his breathing, rhythm and on drawing in energy. As he did, he was able to shift his thinking from a tense, "I've got to get a hit," to a more inspired, "I love to hit the ball." Ray got the key hit. Then a couple more, including a home run in the seventh and final game. He was chosen the World Series most valuable player.

Experiment with the "breathing keys" for yourself. As you do, you may discover that breathing is fundamental to feeling inspired, being in control, and to experiencing high-level performance.

The same breathing basics of tuning into rhythm and inspiring can be beneficial to all performers. Salespeople, like athletes, can benefit by bringing more ease to their process and empowering themselves.

Barry was a commission salesman who sold with an "I've got to" attitude. His desire to excel and his lack of esteem caused him to push and press too hard. His pressing caused prospective buyers to withdraw but their withdrawal made Barry press even more. The result was a high-tension, low-performance avoidance dance.

What Barry required (and received) was more than just feedback on his sales technique. Since we noticed that he would cut down his breathing under pressure, we spent time working with his breathing. What especially helped him was learning to take a breath and draw *in* power whenever he felt "challenged." That simple response of replacing an aggressive surge with a breath and the reminder, "I'm okay. I don't need to close a sale to feel good about myself," and "I have a personal connection to abundance," gave Barry a healthier perspective, more balance, and more ease. It allowed him to think service and "What can I do for *you*" instead of "This is what I've got to have." His customers began to feel more comfortable, and his performance improved.

Remember that you have a personal connection to an unlimited supply of energy and good ideas. With each breath, feel yourself drawing on that resource.

- Inspire yourself. Take six breaths.
- As you breathe, focus on the inbreath.
- With each inbreath feel yourself drawing in energy and power.
- You have a connection to an unlimited supply.
- With each outbreath release tension and negativity.
- Release the outbreath: don't push it out.
- To inspire yourself, focus on the inbreath.
- With each breath, reaffirm your aliveness and direction.
- With each breath, experience power and ease.

Hitting a baseball, selling a product, performing a service, and most other complex activities require a balance of focus and ease.

Tensing, becoming impatient, and pushing too hard may all be understandable behaviors of a motivated player in an achievement-oriented society. However, when these behaviors become habits and interfere with natural response patterns like breathing, they limit performance and well-being. Relax and breathe.

■   ■   ■   ■   ■

TRAINING NOTES

Here's some coaching input for inspirational breathing.

1. As you take your daily five- to ten-minute "breathing session," feel yourself drawing in (breathing in) energy. First, pick up your rhythm; then focus on the inbreath.

2. Starting on week two: at least three times a day, take half a dozen inspirational breaths: focusing on the inbreath—on drawing energy to you.

3. Repeatedly, throughout the day, inspire yourself. Develop the habit, especially when you're feeling stressed or pressured, of tuning into your breathing rhythm and consciously breathing in energy. Remember, *use* stress as a stimulus to draw in power.

4. Thought and breath work together. As you breathe, remind yourself:

• "I have a personal connection to an unlimited supply of energy, possibility, and good ideas."

- "With each breath, I feel more calm, connected, and powerful."
- "I'm the boss."
- "I inspire myself."

Inspiring yourself is the beginning of exercising greater response-ability. Begin with this breath right now.

CHAPTER EIGHT

CONTINUITY

Have you ever lost your focus during an important meeting or event? Continuity is about maintaining order and flow. One way to experience more continuity and consistency is to tune into your breathing.

As a rookie in the big leagues, Sid was a very talented young pitcher who was somewhat erratic and easily upset. He wanted something to enhance his concentration and consistency and help him feel more relaxed while he was on the mound. We began working with his breathing, especially continuity, and the idea that the breath is like waves in the ocean and the waves never stop. Whatever was happening, I wanted him to experience that the waves keep on flowing. When he threw a strike, there was the next wave. If he missed on a pitch, there was the next wave. *Regardless of circumstance or outcome*, whether he was up by a run or down by three, whether he had walked the last batter or struck him out, the waves just kept on rolling. It was wave after wave, breath after breath, and that flow was with him.

During a three-month period, we spent eight or nine hours working together. The coaching addressed power thinking, releasing tension, experiencing the breath as waves in the ocean, and relating this to his pitching. I encouraged him to tune into his breathing from time to time throughout the game. As someone who grew up near the ocean, he enjoyed the wave metaphor and found it useful. The more he tuned into the consistency of the waves, the more ease and consistency he seemed to have on the mound. That year, the waves kept rolling as Sid led the major leagues in strikeouts per innings pitched.

Cam was a Mountie. He had been with the force for about 10 years when he volunteered and was accepted to a "tryout-training camp" for the RCMP's crack antiterrorist unit. This was a super-elite group; selection meant surviving a grueling training process designed to test and push the candidates to the limit. Cam knew the camp would be rough going, so he sought me out for some psychological input to help him successfully meet the intense challenge.

We met only once for about two hours immediately prior to Cam's departure. In that limited time, I wanted to give him something that would be useful, something that he could actually apply under pressure. So I coached him to use his breathing for greater energy, for continuity, and to change doubt and the thought "I can't," into something positive and productive.

Cam reported that camp was brutal. One way to stress people and break them down is to exhaust them, to overload them physically and mentally and see where cracks develop. From dawn to dark the candidates were pushed and prodded to do more. They were asked to run, sprint, do push ups, climb ropes, carry classmates on their backs, and then sprint some more. They were harassed and harangued. Exhausted, they were pushed through obstacle courses, classroom lectures, and psychological situations where they were instructed to observe a scene, then subjected to more intense exercise, and later asked to recall in detail the specifics of what they had seen hours before. After grueling workouts, they were told to dress formally for dinner, then, before eating, told to change and be in full combat gear minutes later. Day after day, they were pushed, hassled, embarrassed, and told they were inadequate and had to do better.

People broke down. Most didn't make it. Physically, they blew out knees and backs. Some quit mentally. A few survived. Afterwards, Cam related that he felt the pressure early on. On Day Two, hurting and tired, he noticed he was becoming negative and self-critical. He started to think, "Maybe I'm not good enough," and "I'm not going to make it."

When he realized what he was thinking, Cam remembered to tune into his breathing and to tell himself, "The waves keep rolling," and "The force is with me." As he tuned into the rhythm and continuity of his breath he felt a surge of energy and the sense that he could go on. At that moment he began to enjoy the challenge.

Continuity is the third breathing key. It's the ability to experience a constant, unending flow of energy. Experience it for yourself. First, make yourself comfortable. Then take *20* breaths.

- As you do, connect your inbreath to your outbreath.
- Connect your outbreath to your inbreath.

- Experience your breath as a continuous flow of energy, in and out.
- On the inbreath, feel yourself drawing in positive energy.
- On the outbreath, feel yourself releasing tension, fatigue, or negativity.
- Feel energy flowing to you and through you.
- Wherever you are, whatever you are doing, tune into your breathing. It can be a source of tremendous strength. The force is with you.

It can be a source of tremendous strength. That force is with you.

As an NFL cornerback, Leroy saw himself as "a man on an island." "I'm on my own out there," he explained. "Everybody can see me but no one can help me." His job involved the high-pressure, high-profile task of covering some of pro football's fastest and best receivers. A mistake, a lapse, a slip could mean a touchdown, or even the game for the opponent. To my mind, it's one of the most demanding jobs in pro sport. Leroy asked me for something that might give him an edge and keep him loose, something that would help him deal effectively with the pressure, play after play. We developed a program and reinforced it with CDs. It was simple. Techniques have to be simple to be useful and effective under pressure.

His program was about experiencing the continuity of the breath. Between plays, no matter what the score, or how much time was left in the game, no matter who he was covering, or what had happened on the last play, Leroy would tune into his breathing. He would specifically focus on the continuity and power of the waves. Between every play Leroy would remind himself to draw on the power of the waves. His experience was that, play after play, breath after breath, the power was there for him. And the thoughts that he combined with his breathing were "I'm in charge," and "The force is with me."

Leroy's ability to focus on his breathing between plays enabled him to reorganize and recharge after an all-out sprint down field or a bone-jarring tackle. It gave him power and consistency. It reduced the interference and stress. It allowed him to play his game. In the two years we worked together, Leroy was a defensive standout and an NFL All-Pro. In a press interview he described our work like this: "My major problem throughout my career (seven seasons) has been consistency and Saul got me into my inner self. He developed *the wave* for me. Got me into watching waves time and again. You know they're so constant and consistent."[1] And so was his play.

Focusing on the continuity of the breath is an age-old prescription. In Japan, about one hundred and fifty years ago, there was a well-known wrestler named Onami (which means "great waves"). According to legend, Onami was very strong and knew the art of wrestling. In his private matches, it was said he even defeated his teacher. In public, he was so shy and uneasy that even his own students threw him. Onami felt that he should go to a Zen master for help. It just so happened that a wandering teacher was stopping at

1. Leroy Irvin, *Los Angeles Herald Examiner*, December 4, 1986.

a little temple nearby, so Onami went to see him and told him of his trouble. "Your name means great waves," said the teacher. "Stay in the temple tonight and imagine you are those waves. You're no longer a wrestler who's afraid. You are like huge waves sweeping away everything before them, swallowing up everything in their path. Do this and you will be the greatest wrestler in the land."

The teacher went to bed. Onami sat in meditation trying to imagine himself as waves. He thought of many things. Gradually his mind turned more and more to his breathing and the feeling of waves. As the night advanced, the waves became larger and larger. They swept away everything in the temple. Even the Buddha in the shrine was inundated. Before dawn the temple was nothing but the ebb and flow of an immense sea.

In the morning, the teacher found Onami meditating. There was a faint smile on his face. He patted the wrestler's shoulder. "Now nothing can disturb you," he said. "You are these waves. You will sweep away everything before you." The same day Onami entered the wrestling contests and won. After that, no one in Japan was able to defeat him.[2]

In addition to surfing the breath, another way you can experience the power and continuity of the breath is to relate breathing to the turning of a wheel.

As you breathe, the wheel turns. On the inbreath, like a clock, it turns up from 6 to 12.

---

2. Adapted from Paul Reps, *Zen Flesh, Zen Bones*, Charles E. Tuttle Inc. Publishers, 1957.

Figure 8.1: Wheels and Waves

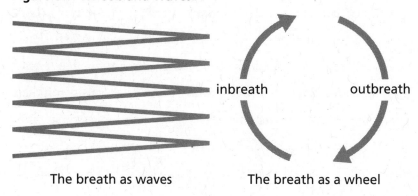

The breath as waves   The breath as a wheel

As you breathe out it turns down, from 12 to 6. Experience your breath as an endlessly turning wheel. As the wheel turns it generates energy. The heart pumps that energy throughout the body. To experience continuity, take 20 breaths connecting your inbreath to your outbreath. Turn the wheel. Generate power. Transform stress and dis-ease into power and ease. Empower yourself. Relax, breathe, and think, "The wheel keeps turning. The waves never stop."

> *"If a person is living out his destiny, he knows everything*
> *he needs to know. There is only one thing that makes a*
> *dream impossible to achieve: a fear of failure."*
> Paulo Coelho, *The Alchemist*[3]

One of the most limiting emotions for any performer is fear. It can be fear of failure, fear of embarrassment, fear of the unknown,

---

3. Paulo Coelho, *The Alchemist*, Harper Collins, 2006.

fear of not meeting your expectations or the expectations of others, and even fear of success. Whenever any of my clients experience limiting thoughts or feelings, I encourage them to *use the emotion* they're feeling *to release tension and turn the wheel.* Focusing on their breathing, they are better able to change anxiety and adversity into power and to be more in charge of the situation. Whenever you experience a negative thought, or find yourself in a difficult or anxiety-producing situation, transform the tendency to tense and contract by tuning into your breathing, turning the wheel, generating more energy, and moving forward.

A phenomenon I have observed too frequently in sport occurs when a winning athlete or team becomes defensive trying to hold on to and protect the lead. The reality is that it's easier to be aggressive than it is to hold on. Holding on is a defensive mindset and trying to hold on is a tensing energy drain. One solution is to go back to the waves; another is turning the wheel.

Jim was a fine pitcher with the Seattle Mariners: the ace of the staff. The two years we worked together were two of his best. One day I was watching him pitch against the Oakland A's, and he was doing great. He had a perfect game through six innings. In the top of the seventh, Oakland's leadoff batter hit a single... and something shifted.

Now the hit itself wasn't important. A double play erased the runner. However, something changed. Instead of pitching with a smooth rhythm and apparent ease, Jim began to take more time. He looked less comfortable; more nervous and fidgety. His pitch selection also changed. Instead of going at the hitters directly with his fastball, he started to throw more change ups and breaking balls and to pitch around them. He survived the seventh inning still leading 1 to 0. But then in the eighth, he lost it. The A's scored a bunch of runs and Jim was taken out of the game, which the A's ultimately won.

I met with Jim two days later and asked him about the performance. "Did anything change for you after that hit in the seventh?"

"Not really," he replied. "Some people said I changed my pitch selection and threw more breaking balls, but I don't think I did."

Then I asked him if he had changed his thinking in any way after the hit. He thought about it for a few seconds, then said, "Well, maybe I did. Before the hit I was into it. I was feeling good. I was relaxed and throwing strikes. After the hit, I guess I tightened up a little and began to think, 'There's only nine outs to go.'"

It was when Jim changed his focus from being aggressive and in the present (from this breath, this pitch) to worrying about holding on to the lead (only nine outs to go) that he slipped out of the moment, out of the groove, lost his edge, and lost the game.

We all slip out of the groove from time to time. It's often the same push to excel, and the same fear of failure that causes us to tense, effort, and stress too much. If this happens to you, if you find yourself pressing, squeezing too hard, slip back into the waves. Focus on feelings of ease and power, and bring those feelings to your performance.

"Nothing external to me can have any power over me."
Walt Whitman[4]

In neuro-linguistic programming (NLP), there's a process called *anchoring* that is used to help people perform in a variety of high-pressure situations. Essentially it involves remembering positive feelings you've had associated with doing something well and connecting these feelings to a physical action that you can use in a pressure situation to elicit those positive feelings. For example, you might recall specific feelings of competence and confidence you experienced after successfully completing a certain task (e.g., making a good golf shot, completing a project, or closing a sale). When you have clear recall of this feeling, you are instructed to do something physical, like squeeze your thumb. You may be instructed to repeat that process several times and/or to recall another empowering feeling memory and squeeze the thumb, again.

The idea is that pairing a powerful positive feeling with a simple physical response (e.g., thumb squeezing) will connect the two. With repetitions, the connection is strengthened and the empowering feelings are anchored and become more accessible. Thereafter, whenever you are in stressful circumstances, making the simple physical response will bring to consciousness the empowering feelings you've anchored and help you to perform under pressure. In my experience, pairing powerful

---

4. Walt Whitman, *Bartlett's Familiar Quotations.*

feeling memories with touching my chest and taking a breath is an effective way to "anchor" positive performance-enhancing feelings.

It's often the same push to excel, and the same fear of failure that causes us to tense, effort, and stress too much. If this happens to you, if you find yourself pressing, squeezing too hard, and worrying, release and breathe. (If you want to use an anchor, touch your chest and take a breath; then think "I can handle this."). Focus on feelings of ease and power. Bring those feelings to your performance.

Here are two ways to strengthen feelings of power and ease and the attitude that goes along with them. First, from time to time throughout the day, be aware of releasing tension and breathe easy; experience a momentary timeout to release and center. Second, take a short power break. That's five to 10 minutes of tuning into your breathing, releasing tension, and focusing on some calming, empowering personal thoughts.

I usually recommend that my clients take a brief power break every day during their season. In sport, the season can last six to eight months. In business it can be all year long. The release reflex and the power break are two ways to reinforce calming, nurturing, and feel-good feelings that enhance performance. They work together. The more you experience and work with the longer process, the better able you'll be to use the release reflex to change channels instantly under pressure. Either way, release... breathe... and focus on feelings of power and ease.

Remember, your motivation to succeed is energizing. The drive to excel can either give you an edge or it can stimulate you to push and squeeze too hard and thus be limiting. In Chapter 6, I described a Dodgers pitcher in a slump. He was a well-motivated, intelligent professional with 10 years of experience in the major leagues, yet, after a string of unsuccessful appearances, he began to experience the pressure to perform as overwhelming. One of the things that helped him to regain his confidence and composure was refocusing on feelings of power and ease. It provided a focus of something other than what could go wrong. And his performance improved dramatically.

To insulate yourself from the limiting, stressful properties of pressure invest a little time everyday tuning into feelings of power and ease. After all, you deserve to feel good And, you deserve to express all of your ability.

Waves of Power: A Review

Conscious breathing is basic to consistent high-level performance. In most of the performance training and seminars I do, I spend a few minutes reviewing the conscious breathing keys. I find that just talking about breathing brings more ease and clarity to the moment.

At an interlude in a performance seminar I was approached by an older gentleman who introduced himself as a banker. "I've always thought that qualities like patience, focus, and controlled aggression are essential to being a good negotiator," he said. "I've read many books and attended innumerable seminars and conferences on the subject and I'm clear that none of that input is any more relevant or more helpful than the breathing techniques you just described. They're basic."

I thanked him for the feedback. Then I reminded him that there was one more essential to making the breathing keys work. "It's important to remember to *use them* throughout the day and especially when you're under pressure."

Breaking That Tensing Habitual Stress Factor

Remember that people tend to perform under pressure as they have previously performed under pressure in the past, unless they over-train themselves at a lower level of emotional intensity. In other words, to break a habit or pattern of tensing or choking under pressure, practice creating feelings of ease in low-arousal situations. This can be accomplished by practicing relaxed, rhythmical breathing in non-threatening situations for a few minutes every day. With practice and time, these new feelings of ease will become firmly established in your behavioral repertoire and you will be better able and more likely to experience more ease and power in pressure situations you encounter.

I recommend to all clients a minimum five minutes of conscious breathing everyday, touching on all three breathing keys (rhythm, inspiration, continuity). Regularly experiencing a relaxing, empowering session of conscious breathing builds confidence, calmness, and power, and will pave the way for a more effective and consistent performance in any situation.

Breathing for Doing... and Being

We have just discussed how rhythm, inspiration, and continuity, three keys to conscious breathing, can help to enhance performance. Some of the performance benefits discussed in the last three chapters: include integrating mind and body, reducing over-thinking and worry, helping to optimize emotional arousal levels, facilitating powering up and calming down, tuning out distraction, releasing tension, refocusing, and enhancing the clarity and quality of thoughts and images basic to power thinking and mental rehearsal.

Meditative breathing is not practiced primarily to enhance performance. Breathing meditation transforms consciousness. It helps shift perspective from a state of striving to a state of being where there is no doing or struggle to achieve. It's as renowned mindfulness meditation teacher and best-selling author Jon Kabit-Zin has said: "The funny thing about stopping is as soon as you do it, here you are."[5]

There are many approaches to meditation. A simple description of one form of breath meditation is as follows: while sitting still, bring your attention to your breath.

Experience the breath flowing in and out.

As thoughts come to mind, notice them, let them go, and gently bring your attention back to the breath.

The breath is like waves in the ocean.

Over time, the waves can wash away tension.

---

5. Jon Kabit-Zinn, www.quotes.net/authors/Jon Kabit-Zinn.

Over time, thoughts lessen, and you experience inner peace.

Meditating removes us from "the race," that sometimes seemingly endless pursuit of doing. It promotes inner peace and a sense of connectedness to all things, and an awareness of "being" as opposed to "doing". Research has also indicated physiological benefits of meditation: reduced heart rate, lower blood pressure, and increased respiratory efficiency.

Conscious breathing, like positive focus, is fundamental to improving performance and quality of life.

■   ■   ■   ■   ■

TRAINING NOTES

Coaching Continuity

1. As part of your daily five- to 10-minute breathing session, experience the "wave after wave" quality of the breath.

2. During week three: at least two or three times a day, take 20 "connected breaths." As you do, experience yourself consciously connecting the inbreath to the outbreath... the outbreath to the inbreath.

- To reinforce the concept of continuity, experience your breathing: as being like waves in the ocean...and like turning a wheel.

- Determine which image of "connecting" the breath, the waves or the wheel, is more energizing or more relaxing for you. Then use that thought to give you a greater sense of ease and power whenever it feels appropriate.

3. Some thoughts to combine with feelings of energy, continuity, and flow:

- "The waves keep rolling."
- "They can wash anything (tension, tiredness) away."
- "Turning the wheel generates power."
- "The force is with me."

CHAPTER NINE

STREAMING

Everyone wants to be more powerful and effective. Streaming is about using energy effectively. It's about channeling the flow of energy to any part of your body and out into the world around you. You can direct or stream your energy internally (within the body) or externally.

Streaming can be a 10- to 20-*minute* process in which you sit or lie back, breathe easily, release tension, and guide energy through the body. The body is like a rechargeable battery. And streaming is a relaxing, recharging, regenerative process.

Streaming can also be a 10- to 20-*second* process in which you release, breathe, and send your energy out. As such, it's an instantaneous, energizing, stress-reducing preparation to excel.

Downhill racers are an interesting breed. The good ones have the ability to be both aggressive and loose at the same time. Gary told me a story of skiing in Europe. He was racing down a slope in Switzerland, hitting speeds of 60 to 70 miles per hour, when his binding popped loose and his ski flew off. "What did you do?" I asked.

"I had a great time going," he replied casually, "so I tried to finish the race on one ski."

When I first met Gary, he was a member of the Canadian ski team. He was a very talented, motivated young man in outstanding physical condition. However, he was experiencing a great deal of leg fatigue on the long downhill courses and it significantly interfered with his performance. He had become so frustrated and depressed about his inability to compete that he considered quitting. The medical team had checked him out and he scored as one of the best-conditioned athletes on the team. He was referred to me for consultation. After talking with Gary and doing some psychological testing with him, it seemed to me that he had two issues. One, he was pressing too hard. Two, his mind and body weren't in synch. It was as if he were thinking at 120 mph and moving at 50.

I began by teaching Gary to relax. We started with conscious breathing and tension-release. As Gary began to breathe more easily and let go of some of the tension, I suggested he do some streaming. He practiced drawing in energy and sending it out through the body, especially sending it down through his legs and feet.

With practice, Gary understood how to use the release principle and streaming to be more at ease and "power full." As he began to exercise more control of his body and to release, breathe, and stream, his leg fatigue disappeared. His confidence grew. Ease and joy returned to his skiing. His endurance increased and Gary gave up thoughts of an early retirement. He continued to race internationally for another five years.

Streaming

As with most things, the best way to learn streaming is to do it.

- To begin, make yourself comfortable and tune into your breathing.
- Pick up the three keys: rhythm, inspiration, and continuity.
- Now scan your body and release any unnecessary tension.
- As you move through the body, recall the feeling of letting go.
- Allow your hands, arms, and shoulders to release... and breathe.
- Allow your jaw and face to relax and breathe.
- Allow your chest and abdomen to be free to expand and contract.
- Let go of tension in the crotch, legs, and feet... and breathe.
- With each breath, draw in energy... then send it out through your body.

Send it out to five points: your hands, your feet, and your head. To send it to your hands, breathe in energy. On the outbreath, allow energy to flow out through your chest, shoulders, and arms, down into the palms of your hands and fingers.

Then send energy to your feet: On the inbreath draw in energy. On the outbreath, send or allow that energy to flow down through your pelvis and legs, into the soles of your feet and toes. Think soft feet, "cat's feet."

Finally, send energy to your head: On the inbreath, draw in energy. On the outbreath, allow that energy to flow up along the spinal column, up through your neck into the top of your head and your eyes. Now, close your eyes and relax the place behind your eyes. It helps to calm the mind.

Tension is contraction. As you breathe, release tension and draw energy to you. On the outbreath, send it out, allow it to flow out simultaneously into the hands, the feet, and up into the eyes... like a five pointed star.

Figure 9.1: Streaming – A Five Pointed Star

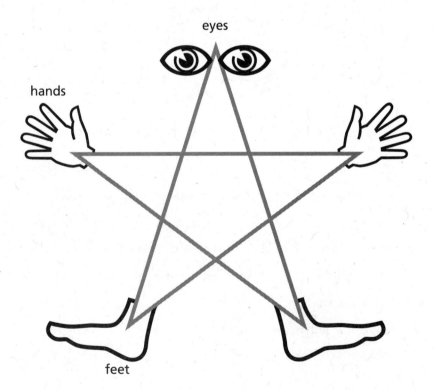

There is great representation for the face, hands, and feet in the sensory cortex of the brain. These are high-awareness areas. As you release and breathe, send energy out to the five points. Allow yourself to experience feelings of ease and power.

Streaming can be used to release tension, to enhance performance, and to reduce pain and promote healing.

Streaming as a Way to Release Tension

The pro football season is six to seven months of physical violence. To stay fresh and alive, one of my clients did some streaming regularly throughout the season. Almost every day he'd put aside 10 to 15 minutes to release and breathe, and stream energy through his body. He invariably had some sore spots (a shoulder, an ankle, a hip, or a thigh) to which he would direct the energy. He found the whole process energizing and recharging.

We used to get together every couple of weeks for a "power session." It consisted of his relaxing and breathing, streaming energy out to the five points, then visualizing himself playing well. As he relaxed, he gradually increased the amplitude of each breath, drawing in more energy and sending more out.

One time when he was breathing rhythmically and inspirationally, he experienced what he called "big waves rolling in." He described feeling wonderful, as if a "sun roof opened up" in the top of his head and golden energy was streaming in and flowing through his body. When he focused on his hands, he described them as "vibrating." He reported feeling so powerful that even though he was relaxed, he felt that if he wanted to, he could punch right through a stone wall. After he had been breathing and streaming for about 10 minutes his energy shifted and he became quiet. He was lying still, and breathing easily and rhythmically. A couple of minutes passed. Then I asked him to relate how he felt on a scale of 1 to 10 (with 10 meaning feeling great). There was a long pause, maybe half a minute; then a quiet voice that sounded far away said, "Ninety." This warrior found streaming a valuable, pleasurable balance to the assault and stress of his occupation. And he used it for years.

The "season" in sales, management, and in most professions can be seen as eleven-plus months of competition, aggression, and stress. You can use streaming as a daily practice to help you to release tension, balance, and recharge, every day.

In the course of competition, athletes often have to react suddenly to stop a ball or puck, or to avoid being hit by something or someone. The tension associated with these intense, contractive reactions is frequently stored in the body. Streaming is a good way for people under pressure to release this stored tension. Be aware that the process of releasing... breathing... and streaming can produce some twitching as the stored tension and stress is released. We release some of the tension and stress we accumulate naturally, especially when exercising and sleeping. Streaming is an efficient and pleasurable way to let go even more, and to keep body and mind relatively stress free.

The wife of an NHL goalie described that sleeping with her husband was like sleeping in a war zone. Between his releasing tension naturally (twitching), and his blocking shots in his dreams, she was getting pummeled. Streaming every day during the season helped him clear some of that tension, and allowed both of them to experience more peaceful, restful sleep.

All of us accumulate and hold tension throughout the day. Just getting to and from work can be tensing and stressful. After a rush hour drive through Los Angeles, one of my NHL clients commented, "How do people put up with this every day? I get more uptight driving around L.A. than by playing an entire hockey game."

Streaming can be very relaxing. I recommend it as daily therapy, anywhere from 20 seconds to 20 minutes a day, whatever feels right to you.

Streaming as a Way to Enhance Performance

Power and flow are two qualities of peak performance. One way to increase power and flow is to slip into the rhythm of the breath, draw in energy, and then direct energy to flow out to your five points. It's a way to build confidence and competence. The pitcher on the mound picks up an inanimate object, a ball, and by directing his energy, throws it right to the target. The golfer or the batter does the same, projecting energy outwards and driving the ball. For a salesperson, directing energy externally may take the form of sending their energy out in the form of an idea or concept to a client or customer. In each instance, the performer is more effective and consistent if he or she is first able to direct energy internally before projecting that energy out to the desired direction.

As the batter stands at the plate, to get a hit it's essential that he see the ball clearly and that he bring his energy (through his bat) to the ball. To do that, I coach him to prepare in the on deck circle by breathing in energy and directing it out to his feet, hands, into the bat, and up into his eyes. I encourage him to feel his power, then bring that energy to hitting the ball.

Bruce was a talented young man who was frustrated by his inability to express his considerable potential. As a collegiate baseball player, his performance had been mediocre. In his first two years at the university, he hit a total of 14 homeruns, had a .230 batting average, and was well on his way to setting a school strikeout record. He was so frustrated by his lack of success that he often upset himself and threw something (a bat or helmet) after one of his strikeouts. Bruce was referred to me by one of his coaches to "help him realize his potential."

When I began working with Bruce, he was a strong man who tried to hit the ball out of the park every time he was at bat. The first thing I did was remind him to release tension and breathe. Then we worked on directing his energy. Like many strong people, he thought his strength was all in his upper body. When he tried to "muscle" the ball, he did it with his shoulders and arms. What helped him was learning to ease up and direct energy out into the bat. (When a batter is tight and squeezes too hard, energy doesn't flow into his bat. Similarly, when a golfer presses and squeezes too hard, less energy flows into the club.) What also helped Bruce was becoming more aware of his lower body. He accomplished this by directing energy down into his feet and developing a greater awareness of his base.

Another valuable training insight Bruce experienced was the sense of tapping into an unlimited supply of energy. The more he relaxed and opened up to it, the more energy he could draw in and direct through his body; the more power he felt, the better he performed. We combined conscious breathing with Bruce's imagining swinging the bat with ease, making good contact, and hitting the ball with power. He imagined himself hitting all kinds of pitches. First we worked with fastballs, then with curves and change ups, pitches which demanded more patience and control. And it all seemed to help. That year, Bruce tied the NCAA record for the most homeruns hit in a single season (a 300 percent performance increment over his previous years' statistics). He led his team to the college world series and was an All-American selection.

When he was interviewed on television late in the season, Bruce was asked, "How is it you're hitting all these homeruns? Have you been lifting weights? Did you change your diet? What are you doing differently?" With a big sweep of his hand he said, "You see, there's this energy all around us. I just open up and let it flow through me." For this strong man, "muscling" and "squeezing" gave way to a process of breathing, easing, and streaming energy. To my mind, Bruce's adjustments were as much mental as they were physical. They involved his realizing that he had a personal connection to an unlimited supply of energy, tapping it, streaming energy, and expressing that power.

Many of my clients are executives. Some wear ties that symbolically separate their heads from their bodies. Streaming can help them to feel more integrated and "connected" both to an unlimited supply of energy and an unlimited supply of good ideas.

After delivering a seminar on Why Teams Win to a group of corporate managers, I was approached by a young woman. She introduced herself as a project manager and explained she had recently been promoted to a challenging position and was very motivated to do an excellent job. Her problem, as she described it, was that shortly after taking on this new position she noticed that she was "running out of energy" and getting very tired over the course of the day. She said it never happened before. She wondered if I had any suggestions as to what was happening to her now and if there was something I could recommend to help her maintain her energy level and her effectiveness throughout her day.

Since she related the onset of the problem to taking on the challenging, new position, I suggested that she might be operating with less confidence than before, and with something of a "don't make a mistake" mindset. I explained that it is both stressful and tiring to be trying to avoid failure. It is much more energizing to be thinking and operating with an "I love the challenge" attitude. I recommended she affirm that she was a capable, competent individual who was good at her job and who loved the challenge it provided. Along with making that shift to more positive, power thinking, I suggested she do a few minutes of streaming a couple of times a day.

When I followed up with her two weeks later she reported that she was following my recommendations and she was feeling more energetic.

Experience it for yourself. Take a moment to tune into your breathing rhythm. Focus on drawing in power. Then stream energy out to the five points. Bring that feeling into whatever you're doing.

Streaming as a Way to Reduce Pain and Promote Healing

Pain is part of life for millions and millions of people. Streaming can be an excellent technique to reduce pain. For six years I ran an interdisciplinary clinic treating chronic pain and chronic disability. Along with medical supervision and an active physical therapy program, streaming was one of the many psycho-physical techniques we used.

As part of the clinic's program, I would demonstrate to clients how much control they had over their bodies. After just a few sessions of relaxation training, I'd ask the members of the group to imagine streaming warm energy down into their right hands. We would then monitor the temperature of that hand with biofeedback equipment. What surprised and delighted most of the group was that they could significantly raise their hand temperature just by thinking of sending warm energy into the hand. Some could even cool the hand below their starting temperature by imagining the hand as cold.

Relaxing and directing warmth into the hand actually affects the flow of blood (energy) into the area, increasing the temperature. Similarly, you can stream soothing, healing, relaxing energy into any part of the body, reducing pain and facilitating the healing process. If you are a visually imaginative person, you can increase that effect by adding the dimension of color to the streaming process. Streaming a warm, soft gold or rose-colored energy into the area of dis-ease tends to increase blood flow and relaxation. It produces a softening or easing effect and is most effective for chronic aches and pains. Streaming a soothing cool blue or green is more effective as an anesthetic for numbing or reducing acute pain.

One client I worked with who had lost a leg in a logging accident was experiencing intense stump pain. By relaxing and streaming a numbing, icy blue energy into the painful area, he was able to make his pain "disappear."

Dave was the manager of one of the more technically sophisticated clothing plants in North America. He had developed and was supervising a very expensive, high-productivity system, and he was committed to seeing it work. In the months it took him to make the venture profitable, Dave put himself under considerable pressure. He worked very hard. He thought about his system 18 hours a day. Then he started to experience severe headaches (caused by a constriction of the blood vessels in his head). The headaches were so intense they affected his health and performance and the way he related to others. He knew he should ease up, but he wasn't doing it. That's when I began to work with him.

I showed Dave two techniques. The first was to release... breathe... and refocus. The second was streaming. I encouraged him to take at least 10 minutes, twice a day to release, breathe, and stream a soothing, relaxing energy through his body. When he had a headache, I told him to send a soothing stream of energy into the headache's center behind his left eye. He'd go right to the spot, allow an easing or opening in the area, and then stream a soothing, numbing cool pastel blue energy right into the center of the disease. Dave's motivation and drive to excel remained unchanged. However, as he began to use the "release" techniques regularly, his ability to handle pressure increased, and the headaches diminished.

Streaming can be an effective analgesic. Locate the exact spot where the tension and pain are most extreme. Explore the pain. Determine the size, shape, intensity, "color," and any other of its properties. What we resist often persists, so, instead of fighting, avoiding, and hating your pain, *gently move into it*. Release and breathe. Then stream a healing, loving energy into the center of that spot. The more you can relax and tune into the center of your pain, the deeper you can go into it; the more soothing energy you can stream through it, the more the pain will diminish.

A number of my clients have experienced serious injuries that have caused them a great deal of discomfort as well as a valuable loss of time on the job. Streaming has helped many of them to reduce pain and speed up their recoveries.

I introduced streaming to a Dodgers pitcher. He had been troubled by a sore elbow for which he had received a variety of state-of-the-art physical therapy treatments. After streaming some cool, soothing blue energy through his sore arm for about 10 minutes, he exclaimed, "My arm actually feels like it's vibrating. This stuff is more powerful than ultrasound."

Streaming is a basic physical expression of body/mind power and control. It is also a method of projecting your energy out into the environment. Either way, the very same principles apply. Remember, you have a personal connection to an unlimited supply of energy. To tap it, release... breathe... stream.

■   ■   ■   ■   ■

TRAINING NOTES

- During weeks two and three: at the end of your daily "breathing session" spend three to five minutes streaming energy out to the five points (and anywhere else you want to attend to). During week four: increase the duration of your streaming sessions to 10 minutes a day.
- During weeks two, three, and four: several times during the day, spend 30 seconds to a minute streaming energy through your body. Remember, streaming can be especially effective when you're tense, tight, tired, depressed, or sore.
- Remind yourself: "I have a personal connection to unlimited energy. Energy flows to me and through me. I deserve to feel good. I am response-able to change my feelings."

CHAPTER TEN

BLOWING OFF TENSION—ENERGIZING

I asked David, a successful newspaper owner and executive, what he did when he was under a lot of pressure. He said, "I go for a walk to clear my mind." I received a similar response from Dawn, a social worker in an Inuit community, when we were discussing community response patterns to stress. "When people here feel pressured or stressed they often go for a hike," she said (and that can be at 30 below zero). But sometimes just taking a breath or a break, or attempting to walk off pressure or upset, doesn't get the job done. You have to do something more, first, like blow off some tension.

On the road with the Seattle Mariners in Chicago, I had arranged an afternoon meeting with a pitcher who had consulted with me on several occasions. When I got to his hotel room, I found him in a heated argument with his wife. I waited outside the room for him to extricate himself from the unpleasant exchange.

When it was over, he was visibly shaken. We went back to my room and since he was still upset I said, "Why don't you just sit back, relax, and tune into your breathing."

"Relax. I don't want to relax!" he roared. "My wife's on my back. My ex-wife's on my case, and my kids are bugging me. I've got a splitting headache, and I'm scheduled to pitch tonight." It was clear that he had to vent some of the charge he had built up, before he could feel calm enough for us to get down to business. He went on to rant about assorted family frustrations for another minute or two; then he quieted down, got into his breathing, relaxed, and the session continued.

Sometimes, when someone's really keyed up, simply releasing and breathing doesn't feel right or just isn't enough to dispel the tension. Another way to make balance and get rid of tension, fear, stagnation, or fatigue is to blow some of it off. There are many ways that can be done. The pitcher's explosion was one. However, exploding and acting out are difficult behaviors to control and they can be very hard on relationships.

Blowing off tension can be useful if the pressure of the moment is overwhelming. It is a safety valve procedure that focuses on the exhalation and on being reactive (rather than causative) to what's happening around you. While I find the technique useful for balancing emotion, for both blowing off excesses and energizing or pumping up, it's often beneficial simply to be with the intense emotion and not try to dispel it, just experience it.

Nick was one of the more thoughtful golfers on the PGA tour. Sometimes his thoughts interfered with his smoothness and consistency. He felt uncomfortable. He was tense and anxious and playing tight, so he decided to check it out. To do that he put on a heart monitor and noticed that as he addressed the ball his heart rate began to accelerate rapidly. It went up to a point considered to be well beyond his optimal performance range. Nick devised a way of literally blowing off some of the tension. Taking his club in both hands and holding it in front of him at eye level, Nick would draw in a breath, then he'd lower the club quickly while blowing out hard. Checking the monitor he discovered that by blowing off tension in this way he could actually send his heart rate way down. It also momentarily reduced some of the tension he experienced. Nick would then play the shot while his heart rate was closer to his optimal performance range.

Nick used this procedure before every shot. I thought the procedure was very mechanical and didn't deal with the cause of his anxiety, so I suggested a few modifications. However, it was a routine Nick was comfortable with and he was playing well. And that's the bottom line.

Another approach to blowing off tension that's a little more dramatic is one I borrowed from the martial arts. It involves a focused, explosive expression of energy in the form of a couple of short punches not directed at anyone—rather like punching through an imaginary block of soft corky wood. Each punch is accompanied by a yell. There's a specific way to punch and yell that can be learned with a little coaching. However, the mechanics needn't inhibit you. Any series of six to eight crisp, short, rhythmical punches (synched to the breath, therefore not rushed, and again, not aimed at anyone) accompanied by a deep (from the chest, not the throat) loud, uninhibited yell can not only dispel tension, inhibition, tiredness, and fear—it can be enjoyable. The classic karate sound that accompanies a punch is "*keeii*," but you can use whatever sound feels right or works for you.

A kilo racer is a cyclist who rides three times around a circular track as fast as he can, for one kilometer, against the clock. When you're a kilo racer you have only one chance at each competition to excel. There's only one ride at the Olympics, or the World Championships. There are no practice heats, no two out of threes. To make things even more intense and high-pressure, the whole race takes just over one minute to complete. There's great pressure to make every tenth of a second count. To do that you have to come off the starting line fast, accelerate quickly and smoothly, get up to top speed, and maintain it for a whole three laps.

As race time approaches, the tension builds. Some competitors respond well to pressure. They use it. Others get tight, and reduce their power. For many competitors, pressure builds in the time just before the race or the game. As such, it is ideal time for blowing off excessive tension and getting into the optimal performance-arousal range.

Curt was one of the finest kilo racers in the world. When we first met at the Pan American Games in Venezuela, he was on the way up. "I've been training for months," he said, "and it all comes down to less than 65 seconds. I've got to make sure I'll be there." As part of his mental preparation, we worked with a variety of techniques from high-performance imagery and power thoughts to a punching and yelling karate exercise that would help him to blow off some of the excessive pre-race tension.

In the introduction, I described Curt as a young cyclist at the Olympics. At 19 he was the youngest competitor in the race. Yet he knew exactly what to do to prepare to excel. He was a power man in a power event. He knew how to focus in on the challenge and what to do to reduce tension. A couple of hours before the race, he relaxed and ran through his breathing, streaming, and imagery routine. In the seconds just before the race, as the pressure built and with it Curt's anxiety level, he straddled his bike, tuned into his breathing, got focused, and did a modified punch and yell technique to blow off any excessive tension. Then he drew in a little more power, and took off.

Curt rode a great race in the Olympics, a personal best. He led the field until the last rider beat his time. He won a silver medal.

Drawing the Power Back

Blowing off tension can provide equilibrium. The key in performance situations is to blow off the excess… not the whole charge. After blowing off tension, it's important to build the energy level back to a point where you feel energized, loose, and powerful, and in your optimal performance range.

Individuals differ in perception. The same pressure situation may be perceived very differently by different people. However, a constant is that people perform best when the pressure they feel is neither too high nor too low.

In addition to blowing off tension as a release, clients have found it useful for energizing and pumping up. I work with men and women, athletes and executives who enjoy the opportunity, permission, and feeling of power involved in blowing off tension. It can be an expressive, assertive way to find balance, to calm down and to experience a performance lift. Athletes like Curt have used it to blow off pre-competition tension. Executives have used it to relieve stress and raise their energy level. And factory workers have used it to re-energize during shift breaks.

The supervisor of one warehousing team I consulted with was a fan of the *haka*, a traditional, stylized movement form of the Maori of New Zealand. Originally a warrior-like group posture dance with shouted accompaniment, it has been popularized worldwide as an impressive, energizing pre-game ritual of the New Zealand's All Black rugby team. The warehouse supervisor asked if there was some way we could bring the energy of the *haka* to warehouse work teams. What we did was to assemble the warehouse leadership team in a circle, facing inwards. People were told to stand with feet shoulder-width apart, knees flexed. They were instructed to tune into their breathing and to synchronize their breathing rhythm. As they did, they were directed to begin punching gently at the air in front of them, at waist level, alternating hands with each punch. Each punch was accompanied with the exhalation of a soft "*haaa*" sound. After a series of soft alternate punches to co-ordinate a team rhythm, what followed were 10 strong punches on the exhalation with each member emitting a deep (from the chest, not the throat), loud "keiii" yell with each punch. The two most noticeable results of the exercise were that it raised the energy level of the group, and the participants enjoyed it. Following up with the supervisor, I was told that from time to time the exercise is used to energize work crews with positive results.

I have used a similar exercise with numerous sport teams prior to a match or to raise energy following a break in the action. The effect has consistently been to raise the energy of the group, bring team members closer together, generate a good feeling, and ready the group to perform.

Calming Down

The same super-release principle is applicable to all of us. In counseling, clients have come in at times with a considerable amount of tension and some very strong emotions. The three emotional "biggies" are anger, fear, and sadness. I usually talk with them about their emotions, goals, and circumstances. Then I remind them to relax (to release, breathe, and refocus). Relaxing is a valuable tool for living, coping, and winning.

Sometimes they're ready to explode. Sometimes their inhibition is like a brick wall, limiting them. In either case, I may have them blow off some tension and emotion so they can feel better and operate more effectively.

Art, a 40-year-old businessman, was intensely angry with his partner. We talked about it for a few minutes; then I asked him to relax and breathe. Like the relief pitcher discussed earlier in the chapter, he responded with, "I'm pissed off, and I'm not going to sit back and relax, not now." So I had him go into his anger and express some of it using a modification of the technique I described.

After Art had released some of the intensity, he was able to sit back, relax, and breathe. As he breathed, he felt more comfortable and at ease. In this less emotional state, Art was more positive and better able to deal with his feelings and circumstances. He affirmed this as well as the fact that he didn't need his partner's approval to feel good about himself. We then began to explore something of what upset Art in his relationship with his partner—and how there were similarities to previous significant relationships.

Had Art not blown off a little of the tension and emotion he would have been too uptight, blocked, or charged to use his experience productively. Had he blown off all the tension and emotion he might have experienced a temporary release, but more than likely he would have lost an opportunity to gain some insight and grow his self-awareness.

Balance enhances performance and well-being. Blowing off tension and energizing is a way to make balance.

■   ■   ■   ■   ■

TRAINING NOTES

It can be stressful, unhealthy, and unproductive to suppress or repress your feelings habitually. Having said that, if you feel very angry, depressed, or upset, it is advisable to consult a therapist or counselor before using the blowing off tension techniques described in the chapter. There's a possibility that a regrettable result could be produced by the combination of poor judgment with the intense emotions sometimes expressed in these exercises.

1. During weeks three and four: Find a space where you won't be disturbing anyone. Then count aloud to 10. Counting is a good way to increase your volume and intensity in incremental steps. Start with 1 being moderately loud. Increase the loudness and intensity with each number so that you are literally *roaring* on numbers 8 through 10.

2. During week four, try this method: punctuate each number with a punch. The punch shouldn't be directed at anyone or anything. Instead, as you punch, imagine punching through a block of soft, corky wood. Keep increasing the amplitude of your sound and your intensity.

- Remind yourself, "I'm the boss. I'm the master of my reactions. I can calm myself down or pump myself up. I enjoy expressing my energy, power, and feelings."

4

S E C T I O N

■ ■ ■ ■ ■

ATTITUDE, INDIVIDUAL DIFFERENCES, AND LIFESTYLE

This last section explores three areas that relate to personality and lifestyle that have an impact on performance, well-being, and our ability to handle pressure.

CHAPTER ELEVEN

A WINNING, PERFORMING-UNDER-PRESSURE ATTITUDE

Attitude is a matter of choice.[1]

An attitude is a predisposition to respond. It's a consistent way of behaving that makes it more (or less) likely that certain things will happen. A winning attitude is a way of thinking, feeling, and acting that predisposes us to success. A negative attitude is one that predisposes us to disappointment, dis-ease, and failure. And a performing-under-pressure attitude is one that enhances success in high-pressure situations. Here are three things to keep in mind about attitude:

- Our attitudes color our perceptions and affect our actions.
- Our attitudes are our own. We create them.
- Our attitudes can be changed.

Professional sport appreciates the impact of attitude on performance. When scouting a young prospect, a baseball organization

---

1. Often quoted remark.

considers both physical and psychological attributes in determining who has the potential to become a big leaguer. When I worked with the New York Mets, each player in the organization was reviewed periodically with regard to both their physical and psychological "make-up."

Make-up, a term that describes character, incorporates motivation, commitment, practical intelligence, coachability, confidence, composure, and command. Composure and command relate specifically to how a player deals with and performs under pressure. There are innumerable examples of players with seemingly limited physical skills, who were initially passed over in selection drafts and organizational evaluations, who went on to become stars because of a winning attitude and their mental toughness. There are also many examples of players with superior physical skills who failed to make it because of attitudinal deficiencies.

Attitude is also prized in business recruitment. Annemarie, a talent sourcing specialist, notes, "Most companies choose attitude over skill set." She goes on to say, "That's particularly true in a team setting. A highly skilled person with a poor attitude can be more destructive to team culture than a person with a great attitude and limited skills. People with a good attitude are coachable, and within reason, we can always train skills.[2]"

Many different qualities contribute to a performing-under-pressure attitude. Some of these qualities can be shaped and

---

2. Annemarie Chapman: Personal communication.

strengthened with training. Six qualities I want to review briefly are motivation, commitment, confidence, deserving, mental toughness, and identity. These qualities are not independent entities. They are overlapping and interrelated. Strengthening one key can strengthen others. For example, strengthening motivation enhances commitment, and commitment increases mental toughness.

Figure 11.1: The Qualities of a Winning Attitude

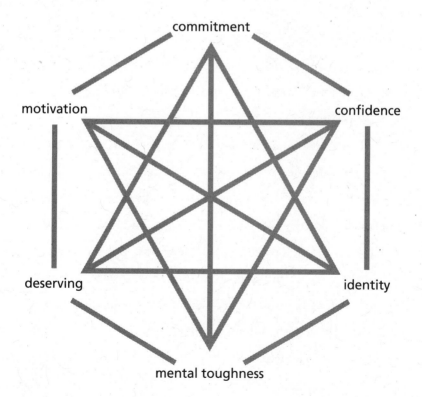

Motivation

Healthy people possess a natural desire to excel. They want to create, achieve, and be a part of something special. Motivation is a driver. As mentioned in Chapter 2, a strong drive to be or do something more can energize us to excellence—or increase pressure, if it isn't well managed. Several factors contribute to motivation being a positive driver that facilitates performance. Three are clarity, meaning, and belief.

Clarity

It's easier and less stressful to get where you are going if you have a clear goal in mind, with a plan of action for getting there. Clarity provides direction and order, and it reduces uncertainty, which many people find stressful.

High achievers in a diversity of fields have reported that when they are overwhelmed by all they have to do, and do well, a simple but effective strategy is to make a list of all the things they have to accomplish, prioritize what's most pressing and relevant, take a few conscious breaths and proceed to tackle what's on the list.

Lists provide clarity and order, but they are not an effective strategy in all circumstances. For example, one of the challenges businesses are facing is satisfying their customers on three interrelated product elements—quality, price, and time. Increasingly, all the screws are being tightened at once. Customers want things done better, faster, and cheaper. As one entrepreneur said, "The pressure can get out of control when I try to deliver on all three of these factors. I can effectively manage delivery on two of the three. We can do top quality inexpensively, but it will take longer. Or, we can do it faster and cheaper, but the quality may not be there. I am genuinely motivated to satisfy the customer. However, I'm really feeling pressured if I'm forced to deliver simultaneously on quality, price, and time." Having clarity with regard to strategy, makes handling pressure more manageable.

Meaning

Select goals that are meaningful to you. Research has shown people will invest more of themselves, will work harder, and endure longer, if what they are striving for is meaningful to them. When that same opportunity is seen as relatively insignificant or meaningless, enthusiasm and energy diminish and performance suffers.

In my book *Why Teams Win: 9 Keys to Success in Business, Sport, and Beyond*,[3] I described receiving a phone call from a veteran professional athlete late in the season. His team had been eliminated from the playoffs and they were playing out the final games of their schedule. During the season he had been plagued by a series of injuries but he was able to put the negatives aside and perform. However, now that his team was out of the running, he complained that the pain and fatigue were overwhelming. "I just don't have the energy or enthusiasm to give 100 percent any more," he said. "I even have trouble concentrating."

---

3. Dr. Saul L. Miller, *Why Teams Win: 9 Keys to Success in Business, Sport, and Beyond*, John Wiley & Sons, Toronto, Canada, 2009, Josey Bass, USA 2009.

I explained that fatigue can sap concentration and enthusiasm. However, it was clear that what he was referring to was more than fatigue. The lack of consequence, his perception of the meaninglessness of the remaining games, lessened his will to compete. Conversely, in the playoffs when success and elimination hang in the balance, players will endure almost any hardship and stay focused. It's the same in business when people are required to deliver on a vitally important project; highly motivated corporate players will press forward despite fatigue, illness, or personal issues. A meaningful purpose is a source of power and an antidote to pressure.

"Champions are made from something they have deep iside them: A desire, a dream, a vision…. They have to have the skill and the will. And the will must be stronger than the skill."
Muhammed Ali

Belief

Winning feels good. As with meaning, people will weather the storm and endure more when they genuinely *believe* winning is possible. Failure is painful and it can be embarrassing. People withdraw their spirit and attachment when they don't believe success is possible. Both power and performance decrease when the thinking is, "What's the use?".

One emotion that limits performance is fear. People fear many things. Some fear failure and what it might say about them. They think of doing as being, and interpret not doing or not succeeding as a statement that they're not okay. To protect themselves from fear and the pain of embarrassment, these individuals unconsciously suppress their desire to excel. This behavioral pattern sometimes shows up amongst individuals in teams that lose repeatedly. In the case of losing in the short term, elite athletes often get upset. However, when losing becomes a habit and belief fades, some develop a negative, defensive attitude characterized by thinking, "Well, it's not my fault. I'm doing my job," and "What's the use?" Of course, they still have to perform, so they go through the motions, but they do it with less determination, drive, and enthusiasm. The negatives around them become magnified. Performance slides.

When we fear something, we contract—we become more defensive and guarded. When we love something, we expand; we gain energy and move into and embrace the challenge. People can perform okay with fear, but they perform at their best with love. *Love is power.* The two easiest ways to love yourself are, first, take time to breathe. (Experience your breathing rhythm. Draw energy to you. Remember, you deserve to feel good. And *you deserve to express your ability*.) Second, say positive things to yourself. Use power thoughts and power images. Be a positive, empowering force. Enjoy the challenge of motivating yourself and others with love. Whatever the task, *love the challenge*.

Commitment

I define commitment as the willingness to do what is necessary to get the job done. It's paying the price. As I see it, if you are committed to being the best you can be (at whatever you aspire to), then you have to *"use"* whatever comes up.

If you don't use it, it will use you. When you are performing well, *use* the success to build confidence. Affirm, "That's who I am." When performance is less than desirable, use the feedback to sharpen your process. Winners use everything.

Cathy was an intelligent, sensitive Olympic gymnast who was the subject of her Russian coach's frequent, loud, negative feedback. Cathy felt the coach's critical diatribes were counterproductive, and asked what she could do to deal with the coach. I explained to Cathy that if she was genuinely committed to being the best she could be, then her only option was to use the coach's negativity and criticism to strengthen her identity as a more centered, confident performer. I asked her, "Why does the coach yell at you? Why is he so critical?"

After some reflection she said, "I guess it's because he knows I can do it."

"Exactly," I replied. "In yelling at you he is telling you that you can. If he didn't think it was possible for you to execute the routine, he wouldn't yell. A more sensitive person might realize you would perform better if the feedback was more positive and supportive. However, he is who he is."

Then I suggested to Cathy that she define the specific actions she wanted to manifest on the apparatus, that she continue to work hard in practice to execute these actions (preparation builds confidence), and that she acknowledge herself when she performed well.

"If you do the routine well, say, 'That's me. That's who I am.' If you do it poorly, say, 'No way, that's not me,' and visualize yourself doing it well." I reminded Cathy that if her commitment was to be the best, she had to use it all. I encouraged her to realize and affirm, "I don't need the coach's approval to feel good about myself." And similarly, "I don't need him not to yell for me to perform well."

Roy, a highly motivated insurance advisor, put a lot of pressure on himself to lead his sales team in written business. He came to see me for what he described as "some tension headaches and a few temper outbursts," that he attributed to clients who were indecisive and unresponsive to his presentations. He said, "They make me so angry I could blow my top." He wanted to know how he could deal with his frustration.

I suggested to Roy that if he was genuinely committed to being the best he could be, he should learn to *use* the situation and these clients to be less reactive, feel better about himself, and improve his presentations. I explained, "The clients you find so frustrating are giving you a message. They are there to assist you to improve your process and your well-being."

First, I helped Roy to relax... and breathe consciously. We discussed the importance of creating ease instead of dis-ease. I reminded Roy that he, not his clients, was response-able for his thoughts and feelings. Then we explored why he was so driven to be number one, and why if someone didn't respond favorably to a presentation he would become so upset. I explained the difference between preference and addiction, and helped Roy to understand how an "I've got to close" (this sale) "attitude is more pressure- and anxiety-driven (and ultimately less effective) than is an "I love to communicate these excellent opportunities." After discussion and reflection, Roy was willing to affirm, "I'm an intelligent, capable, caring individual. And I don't need some client to agree with me, or appreciate me, or buy insurance from me, to feel good about myself."

I reiterated that if Roy was committed to being the best advisor he could be he should *use* his clients' responsiveness or lack of response to enhance his preparation. I related the Japanese concept of *kaizen*, a commitment to continuous improvement, and suggested Roy use upset as a stimulus to improve his knowledge of product, his research of the client, and his ability to prospect their needs.

Assess and adjust is the mantra for self-improvement. Commitment is the willingness to do what's necessary to achieve our goals. That willingness is a force. It's been said that the moment we totally commit ourselves then providence moves too, and with it all sorts of things begin to happen to help us that would never otherwise have occurred to move us closer to our goal.

Commitment can be nurtured. One of the teams I was involved with had the formidable challenge of having to win the gold medal at the Pan American Games in order to qualify for the Olympics. The pressure was intensified by their sporting association's belief that if they didn't win gold they would lose funds vital to the support of their program. The president felt that the team had the talent and coaching to win. However, since they had never won the gold medal before, he asked me to help them to develop a winning attitude. I thought one step in building that winning mindset was defining a clear goal; the second was getting the players to commit to achieving it.

I traveled with the team for several weeks working on basic mental skills. Then I addressed their beliefs and commitment directly. At a training camp about a month before the Games, I asked the players to read the following "Statement of Commitment and Intent":

"It is my intention to win a gold medal at the Pan American games this August. _____ *(initial)* _____ ."

"I _____ *(sign)* _____ *am willing to do whatever is necessary to serve this team and help us to achieve our goal."*

"I _____ *(sign)* _____ *genuinely believe that we are winners and that we can and will win it all."*

"There is nothing to prevent us from achieving our goal of a gold medal." _____ *(initial)* _____ ."

"I _____ *(sign)* _____ *am committing myself to serving the team and winning the gold medal in the Pan American Games."*

Each player was asked to read the five statements carefully. If they agreed with what was written they were asked to sign the statement. They all complied. Next, each player was instructed to read the statement aloud in front of his peers. The teammates were asked to listen and comment on whether or not the reader sounded convincing in expressing his commitment to the team's success. If he didn't, he was asked to reread the statement until his teammates were sufficiently satisfied that his commitment sounded genuine. All sixteen athletes participated. When the camp broke up, everyone was clear that the team's mission was to win the gold medal. And everyone had expressed their commitment to making it happen.

As a parting request the players were asked to memorize the statement so that the next time we met, each individual would be able to recite it to the group. When we met on our way to South America a couple of weeks later, all the players had memorized the mission statement. For the next three weeks, before each team meeting one player was randomly selected and asked to recite the statement of intent. The ritual of starting a meeting with the recitation of the statement of intent and commitment became a meaningful, inspiring (and sometimes entertaining) reaffirmation of purpose.

It's enjoyable to be positive. Some of the players wrote the statement on the walls of their room. Everyone seemed committed to winning. And the team played that way. Nothing is perfect. There were the occasional minor incidents, which we *used* to remind people of our mission. I recall two of our players getting entangled in a shoving match that almost led to blows. I stepped in between them and said, "Remember your commitment to do whatever is necessary to serve the team. This *does not* serve the team." They both agreed instantly and immediately changed channels.

The team won the first six games and, in so doing, qualified for the gold medal game against Argentina, the perennial gold medalist—a team that had never lost a single game in Pan American competition up to that point.

The gold medal game was a battle. It could have gone either way. Actually, the opposition dominated the play. But we won the game and the gold. After the gold medal ceremony the president of the association came over to congratulate me. He remarked that it wasn't that the team played so much better than before. It's just that they didn't believe they could lose. I agreed and replied, "They were committed to winning."

To perform under pressure, first be willing to pay the price, to stay on purpose and do *whatever* is necessary to achieve success. And learn to use the situation (whatever comes up) to move closer to the goal.

Confidence

Confidence means "with faith." It's a knowing and feeling that "I can." It enhances performance and strengthens one's resistance to the limiting effects of pressure. Two things build confidence. The first is success. Confidence comes from having done it before, and having done it well.

The second thing that builds confidence is preparation. If you haven't had that winning experience, if you've never done it, or if you haven't been doing it consistently or lately, one way to strengthen confidence is to prepare for success. That means preparing both mind and body. The formula for building confidence is a combination of positive focus, winning thoughts, and high-performance images, feelings of power and ease, and the physical and skill preparation necessary to excel... plus lots of practice.

Luke was an NHL All-Star winger. When he was playing his best he went to the net with confidence and the sense that he could make the play. If he didn't have the puck, he played as if he knew it would be there for him. When he had the puck on his stick and he was in front of the net, he felt sure he could beat the goalie and score. He didn't think about it; he knew it.

I met him several years later after he had experienced a few serious injuries and been traded a couple of times. He no longer had the feeling. He didn't burst to the net anymore. He didn't expect the pass in front. He was no longer sure he'd beat the goalie and score. He lacked confidence and his play was routine and uninspired.

He came to see me to rebuild his confidence. He was a motivated and intelligent professional who could still skate like the wind. The first thing I did was to teach Luke to release and breathe. I encouraged him to take a "power break" and do 10 to 15 minutes of conscious breathing every day. As Luke relaxed and lightened up, he was instructed to imagine himself playing great hockey. First, he would imagine himself going to the net, taking a pass, shooting accurately, and scoring. Then he'd see himself going to the net, drawing the defenseman, and making a sharp accurate pass. He'd imagine himself executing perfectly, with speed and ease. And he did many repetitions. He'd imagine the same plays again and again. Between each scene, he'd release tension, take a few relaxing breaths, then imagine the play again. Gradually, we expanded the repertoire of plays he would mentally rehearse to include more complexity, and playing under more pressure. He'd release, breathe, create some winning feelings, and then imagine himself making all the plays... and playing great.

We also looked at clearly defining his role. His anxiety and lack of confidence occasionally got him into fights. Fighting was an inappropriate preoccupation. He was a goal scorer, not a policeman. He understood and affirmed that it was essential for him to play his game. When provoked, he was to use the experience, not to retaliate automatically, but to "change channels" and focus on creating scoring chances. We met every 10 days for about three months. Sessions lasted about an hour. Luke was encouraged to spend some time each day doing his homework (breathing, releasing, imagining success, thinking power thoughts, and feeling powerful). Gradually, the feelings, the focus, and the self-image became stronger and more positive. So did his confidence and his attitude about himself. He wasn't the same player he had been years before, but then, who ever is? Previously, he did things instinctively, without thinking about them. Now he used his mind more assertively to create the feelings of power, ease, and competence that lifted his game. Bottom line, the faith was back. He regained his confidence. He was playing well and enjoying (not fearing) the game.

Julie was having a very different confidence problem. She was especially uptight about a presentation on exercise and diabetes she was scheduled to make to a group of physicians at the hospital where she worked. Julie's fears were unreasonable when you consider that she knew her topic very well, she had considerable experience counseling diabetics about the benefits of exercise, she spent hours everyday leading exercise groups, and she had spent months researching the subject of diet, exercise, and diabetes.

We explored what it was about the upcoming presentation that worried her. Since preparation builds confidence, I asked her if her nervousness was caused by a lack of preparation.

"No," she replied, "I think I'm prepared."

"Do you think the doctors in the audience may be more knowledgeable than you about the subject?"

"No."

"Do you think they're likely to harass or embarrass you?"

"No."

"Then what is it?" I asked.

What Julie eventually came up with had to do with her not feeling good about herself. She was concerned that in the pressure of the moment, and in front of what she perceived to be a prestigious authority group, she might do something or reveal some part of herself that wasn't okay.

I began by helping her to relax and breathe, to feel good. As with the hockey player, we reinforced the notion that she deserved to feel good, that feeling good was natural, and that she controlled the switch. Julie practiced releasing and breathing. As she felt more calm and centered, she began to imagine talking about her professional experience of exercise and diabetes. I reminded her that she was a genuine expert with an extensive personal experience of exercise. She imagined describing the benefits of exercise and how it consistently contributed to her feeling well. Then she imagined talking about some of the people she counseled, including those with blood sugar problems who responded well to the exercise programs she prescribed. She added to her presentation some of the research findings she had reviewed.

Julie reported that she was comfortable and confident talking about experiences she'd had working with others. She relaxed and did some mental rehearsal, running through her presentation in her imagination and being well received by the group. Then, to cover every eventuality, I instructed her to imagine the audience being challenging, critical, and even disagreeing somewhat unpleasantly with her. While the thought of being challenged would have been quite threatening earlier, she now found the possibility both unlikely and amusing. Even under these circumstances, Julie reported that she saw herself as calm, breathing, and sharing her expertise and knowledge. She rehearsed her presentation several times.

Julie was prepared and her presentation was a success. She confronted her fear and emerged from the experience feeling better about herself and with a technique for strengthening feelings of confidence should the need arise in the future.

Auditions are especially challenging to performers. Confidence is challenged by the frank reality that *you are being evaluated.* Whether it's an athlete trying to make a team, a person going for a job interview, or an actor or musician looking for work, the challenge to impress often raises tense, anxious questions, like "Am I good enough?"

I was doing a sports talk radio show when a caller phoned to say, "What I do is very similar to some of the sports you've been talking about. It requires a great deal of coordination, the ability to make hundreds of subtle movements, a tremendous amount of teamwork, and being in very good shape. I'm a cellist for the symphony orchestra."

He went on to explain that he was experiencing a dilemma. He had been a regular member of the orchestra for years, playing up to 200 performances in a season. With the impending dissolution of the orchestra, he was now faced with the intense pressure of auditioning for others around North America. What he found at these auditions was 90 to 120 candidates competing for *one job.* The pressure was intense. He described how some of the musicians were using whatever techniques they thought might work to give them a competitive edge, including drugs like beta blockers. He was worried and wanted to know what I might recommend for him.

What makes an audition so challenging is that there's so much emphasis on winning the job. The focus is "outcome" and the future, as opposed to the *process* of playing, and being in the moment. One of the best ways I know to help someone shift from "outcome" into "process" is guiding them into their breathing. (As they tune into the focal point where the inbreath becomes an outbreath, they move back into the moment.)

Since preparation builds confidence, I recommended an audition preparation routine for the cellist. It consisted of his tuning into his breathing and giving himself time for his inbreath to come all the way in. And I directed him to the point where his breath changed direction. I encouraged him to sit quietly and do a minimum of 10 minutes of conscious breathing every day for a week. The next week, I suggested that after five minutes of rhythmical breathing, while holding his cello, he begin to play the instrument while maintaining this enhanced breathing awareness. As his breathing consciousness became more natural, I encouraged him to return his focus to the specifics of playing well: things like the feeling of the bow on the strings, the sensation of bowing and fingering with sensitivity, and playing with clarity and quality of tone. Last but not least, I encouraged him to affirm that he was a very experienced and talented musician, who loved every opportunity to play.

After the telephone call, the sport talk show host mused, "In the 10-year history of the show, we've had calls about everything from baseball to sailing, from football to golf. But that's the first time that someone had actually called to inquire about playing the cello."

I wasn't surprised by the call. I've worked with a number of musicians, singers, and actors as well as athletes and corporate executives. The same aspects of excelling under pressure apply in all theatres of performance.

A Sense of Deserving

Some people feel they deserve success; others don't.

Cliff was a collegiate tennis player who played number four on a good Division 1 college tennis team. I was asked to work with him when his coach observed that he rarely won the first set. The coach also noted that, once Cliff fell behind, he'd play much better. However, the problem was that Cliff simply wasn't a good enough tennis player to consistently yield the first set to his very capable opponents.

When I heard that he started poorly, my first thought was that Cliff was probably too tight going into the match. So I began by addressing the tension and working with Cliff's ability to release and breathe consciously. After a short time, it was apparent that pre-competition tension wasn't Cliff's problem. The issue was that Cliff simply didn't believe he deserved to win. What made matters more interesting was that Cliff was also clear he didn't deserve to lose. The result was whenever he was down he would become more aggressive and play with abandon and impact. What we all wanted Cliff to do was to bring his competitive spirit and drive to his play from the beginning of the match.

Because of time constraints, I chose not to work in depth with Cliff's questionable self-esteem. Instead, we focused on conscious breathing and relaxation. In a deeply relaxed state, Cliff acknowledged that he deserved to feel good, that it was natural. Then, I asked him to imagine himself playing well. As he did, he repeated the thought, "I deserve to express my ability, all my ability." I explained to Cliff that the match was not really about him versus some other guy; it was not about who was better. It was about challenging himself to be the best he could be. I explained to Cliff that his oppoent was simply there to provide him with the opportunity to express his ability, his gift. And he deserved to express it all.

Cliff was able to create the bridge from being to doing; from breathing easily, feeling good, and knowing he deserved to feel good to seeing himself excelling and feeling that he deserved to express his ability. Once he could do that, he never had another problem with the first set.

A strong sense of deserving can strengthen confidence and reduce anxiety and pressure. As you experience your breathing rhythm, take your time and know, "I deserve my time." Extend that sense of knowing and deserving to the idea that you deserve to express your ability. Then refocus and address the situation.

Excellence is a very personal affair. Examine your performance feelings. Take inventory. Define the specific feeling elements that go with your performing well. Think about the feelings you want to experience more of and less of. Be aware of how, when, and where you feel pressure and how you can effectively deal with it. Use your mind assertively to create the feelings you want. Focus on feelings of power, ease, and competence. Remember, your feelings color your thoughts and images. You deserve to express your ability. You control the switch.

Mental Toughness

A great deal has been said about mental toughness.

- Vince Lombardi said, "Mental toughness is essential to success."[4]
- Bobby Knight said, "Mental toughness is to the physical as four is to one."[5]
- Dave "Tiger" Williams said, "Mental toughness is playing like your next effort might be the difference. It's playing like your next effort after that might be the difference. It's playing like every effort you make throughout the game might be the difference. And it's doing it game after game."[6]

Mental toughness is fundamental to dealing effectively with pressure. It means staying tuned into the power channel, no matter what. Mental toughness is not a magical property given by the gods to a select few. As with most skill, performers can develop it with training. Remember, the stimulus you focus on is magnified in your consciousness while the other stimuli competing for your

4. Vince Lombardi, in Ferguson, Howard (ed.) *The Edge*, Getting The Edge Co., Cleveland, Ohio, 1983

5. Bobby Knight, in Ferguson, Howard (ed.) *The Edge*, Getting The Edge Co., Cleveland, Ohio, 1983

6. Tiger Williams, in Dr. Saul L. Miller, *Hockey Tough: Winning the Mental Game*, Human Kinetics, Champaign, IL, 2003.

attention are diminished in your perceptual field. This means that if you focus on difficulty and worry instead of the task at hand, difficulty and worry become magnified in your consciousness. If you focus on the negative consequences of not being successful, those negative consequences become even more significant. In contrast, if you focus on power and possibility, you empower yourself and are better able to persevere.

The mind is our most potent weapon. If you aspire to succeed in life's many challenges, the mind must lead the body. Coaches have repeatedly commented that their best players are those who demonstrate control of mind as well as body.

I was talking to a group of top female divers about mental training. "It's really very simple," I said. "In theory, all that's involved is having a clear idea of what you want to do and then doing it. However, sometimes something can come between the image and your doing it." I asked the group, "What's an example of something that can intrude between the image and the action?"

"Thirty-three feet of air," piped up Paige a, seventeen-year-old 10-meter diver. In her world, mental toughness is leaping out into 33 feet of air, executing her dive routine, and hitting the water cleanly at 60 miles per hour.

Six months later, Paige called me from the World Championships. She had won a gold medal at Nationals in the 10-meter diving competition. Now she was competing at the Worlds.

"How are you doing?" I asked.

"I'm not so sure." she replied.

"What's happening?"

"I'm very nervous."

"What are you thinking? What are you saying to yourself?"

"Well, I tried telling myself it wasn't competition. I thought that if I said to myself it was just practice I wouldn't be as nervous." she continued. "But it doesn't seem to work."

"Well, that's not true." I commented. "It *is* competition." Then I paused, took a breath, and thought for a moment.

"When do you dive next?" I asked.

"In less than an hour."

"How many dives will you do?"

"Four," she replied.

"Do you know what they are?"

"Sure," she answered. "They're my optionals."

"What's the first dive?" I asked.

"It's a reverse two-and-a-half pike."

"Okay. What do you have to do to really excel at that dive?" I asked. "Tell me three things: A, B, C."

"Well, I have to have a good take off, go up and not out. That's A. Then I want to do two really tight summersaults. That's B. And I have to focus on the water and have a clean rip entry. That's C."

"Good; you are very clear. And that's what you want to focus on. ABC," I said. "No matter what's happening or what you may be feeling, before that dive think, imagine, and feel yourself executing your ABCs." Then we moved on to the next dive, and the third. With each dive I helped her define an ABC to focus on.

I advised her not to think of the second dive until she had completed the first. "Keep it simple. Think ABC for the dive you're doing. And that's it. If you feel nervous, or frightened, if you feel like you'd rather be at home, or somewhere else, don't fight it. Use it. Breathe, release, and clear the screen. Then tune into your ABC for that dive." I went on, "You're smart. You're talented. You're well-coached. You've trained hard. And you are mentally tough." Then we returned to the first dive. "Now how well can you score on the first dive?" I asked.

"Nine," she replied, describing a score out of 10.

"Okay," I said. "What do you have to do to achieve a nine out of 10?"

"I have to hit my ABC," she replied.

"Exactly. And that's what to focus on." I said. "You may feel anxious. That's okay. You're mentally tough. You can tune out any distraction. Just breathe easy and focus on the ABC."

Paige performed very well.

Diving can be scary. Diving in the World Championships can be especially frightening. However, a similar process of releasing, breathing, tuning out distraction, and focusing on specific ABCs can help performers build focus and the mental toughness to meet the challenges they may experience at one time or another.

Chuck Noll, the legendary Pittsburgh Steelers football coach, put it nicely when he said, "Some place along in life you are going to have to function in a pressure situation, and if you can learn to do it in a game where the results are not life and death, you can come to a situation where it is life and death and you will be better able to cope."[7]

In his book *Mental Toughness Training for Sports*, psychologist Jim Loehr says, "The extent to which individuals will perform toward the upper range of their talent and skill largely depends on the success they have in creating and maintaining a particular kind of mental climate within themselves."[8] Some of the mental characteristics Loehr lists as necessary for an ideal performance state include: being energetically charged yet relaxed; having a positive state of mind; exhibiting mental alertness, focus, discipline, self-confidence, and control. These are all cornerstones of mental toughness and elements we discuss throughout this book.

Mental toughness is about staying tuned into the power channel. It's practicing the techniques described in this book. Mental toughness is releasing distractions... breathing easily... and refocusing on thoughts, images, words, and feelings that give you power. It's remembering that regardless of circumstances you are the boss. You control what you tune into on your mental TV. Growing a winning attitude is a process of strengthening motivation and commitment, developing your ability to change channels, and learning to use the situation at hand instead of allowing it to use you. As you do, your confidence, self-esteem, and perception of what is possible will also grow.

---

7. Chuck Knoll, in Ferguson, Howard (ed.) *The Edge*, Getting The Edge Co., Cleveland, Ohio, 1983.

8. James Loehr, in *Mental Toughness Training for Sports*, by James E. Loehr, the Stephen Greene Press, New York, 1986.

Identity

A strong sense of self is a foundation for success. It strengthens all the attitudinal elements we discussed and makes us less vulnerable to pressure, stress, and disappointment. If things are not happening as planned, people with a positive identity don't judge themselves negatively. Instead they *use* the experience to discover things to focus on to improve their performance.

The more a performer can see him or herself as a winner, the more likely he or she is to perform that way. In Chapter 2, I mentioned that I frequently instruct clients to see themselves at their best, to talk to themselves as if they are capable, and, to have a clear understanding as to why they are effective performers. Having a strong positive identity enhances confidence, improves performance, and reduces pressure.

Deborah, a publicist, described herself as very capable, explaining, "I maintain strong relationships with my media contacts; I am well organized and very good at handling detail; I am intelligent, responsible, and hard working." Pete, a goalie, responded to the question, "How effective are you?" saying, " I'm very good." When I asked him why, he replied, "Because I'm fast; I have good technique; and I'm focused. Nothing takes me off track." Doug, a respected forestry consultant, explained his effectiveness: "I'm knowledgeable; I work very hard; I am client-oriented; and I'm responsible. I deliver meaningful information on time." Repetition builds strength. I encourage clients to regularly remind themselves that they are capable... and why.

As my clients experience success, I coach them to acknowledge themselves, and to reinforce their capability by saying, "That's who I am." When they perform poorly, I suggest they look at the specific behavior they perceive as being substandard and think, "That's not me." And then I recommend they use the experience to reaffirm the positive, by imagining themselves making a positive adjustment and performing well.

When things are not going well, some people lose perspective on who they are and what they are capable of achieving. Some years ago, I worked with three sprinters at the Pan American Games in Venezuela. The three had flown to South America directly from Finland, where they had competed in the World Championships. Not only had they performed poorly in Finland, but there was also some emotional upset between the three athletes and one of their teammates. They were scheduled to compete three and four days later, and their attitude and prospects were not very good. The team manager asked me to work with them.

When I first met with them they looked tense and tired and they described themselves accordingly. One athlete summed it up by saying, "We're really beat." Of course, that's not a state very likely to produce success. I began by showing them how to ease up. We spent an hour working with breathing and tension release. The next day we spent a little more time relaxing, creating some positive feelings and then pairing those feelings with thoughts like, "I deserve to feel good," and "I control the switch." At our third meeting, the athletes were noticeably more at ease. As they did more relaxation and breathing training, I guided them to combine the good feeling with thoughts like, "I deserve to express my ability." Then, to get them into an even more positive mind-space we began what I call *constructive wondering*. I asked the three women to consider how fast a woman could run the 400 meters under ideal conditions. In other words, what was humanly possible? "Think about it," I said. "If a healthy young woman with all the right physical attributes, wisely trained in her formative years, was very well coached, in great shape, had everything just right for her, how fast could she run the 400 meters?" It was a positive question and one that forced a shift in focus from limitation to possibility. The time they estimated was substantially faster than the world record at that time.

Next, I said, "I know you've said you're all a little tired. However, let's say you wake up tomorrow feeling fine… strong, loose, and fast. And let's say you ran a great race. How good could you be tomorrow?" They smiled and laughed. Their attitudes and their sense of who they were, shifted from "We're tired," to "We're good," with a focus on what was possible.

The result was they all responded with a time that was better than their personal best. In the next two days they all ran great races. One won a gold medal and set a Pan American record in the 400 meters. All three won silver medals in the 4x100 meter relay. Breathing and release, combined with physical training, creative positive thinking, and a winning attitude, are basic ingredients to performing well under pressure.

I am paid to help people perform at their best. For balance and well-being, whenever possible, I counsel clients that they are more than their performance. They are remarkable human beings, capable of experiencing themselves in many ways. And while most of us choose to express our creativity and power through our performance, I believe it is both health- and performance-enhancing to appreciate that we are more than that.

A well-rounded lifestyle provides perspective and balance. Having healthy relationships can insulate us from the negative effects of pressure. Many clients have expressed that being with family and friends is a positive balancing diversion from the pressure to compete and perform. Tiger Woods, discussing the perspective that having children has brought to his game, has said that when he has a bad hole or a bad round he thinks of his children, and it's not as bad.[9] The Greg Louganis comment cited earlier ("Even if I blow this dive my mother will still love me."[10]) similarly reflects the perspective and balance that loving relationships provide.

For others, faith may be a source of perspective and strength. When I worked with the New York Mets, one of my clients was an All-Star and a devout Christian. Initially, he was reluctant for us to work together, until I reminded him that the New Testament begins with, "In the beginning was the word." I explained that *word* can mean thought and breath combined, and thought and breath is exactly what I work with.

---

9. Tiger Woods, Team 1040 radio, May 28, 2009.
10. Greg Louganis, sermonillustrations.com.

He was a very motivated player, renowned for his 100 percent attitude. However, late in his career, his reactions had slowed and to compensate he was trying too hard, tensing, and over-efforting. We worked on his breathing and release but even after some training he was still trying too hard. Watching him over-effort, I said to him, "God's not going to love you more if you get a hit." Instantly he knew he was trying too hard. He smiled, took a breath, and released some of the tension.

In baseball there's an expression, "trying easy." It's something the ball player could approximate by releasing some of his angst to faith. The intense desire to excel possessed by many high achievers can be a positive driving force. However, it can also lead to limiting tension and dis-ease—unless it's managed with a healthy perspective, a supportive lifestyle, and good technique.

A winning, performing-under-pressure attitude consists of having clear, meaningful goals, the positive belief that one's goals are achievable, a commitment to making that happen, the confidence that one can, a sense of deserving, the mental toughness to stay on purpose, and a positive self-image. A winning, performing-under-pressure attitude is a powerful insulation against pressure, and an enormous step towards getting what you want in life.

TRAINING NOTES

A Winning Attitude

Books have been written about the significance of attitude. In an effort to be succinct, I've described six attitudinal elements which specifically relate to performing under pressure. Work with these elements to become more of a high-pressure performer.

1. Week one: Practice breathing and releasing. Think of you at your best. At least once a day, every day, say aloud, "I am a talented individual. I deserve to express my abilities."

2. Week two: Make a want list. Write down at least a dozen things you want to do, be, or accomplish. Create clear, *meaningful* goals. Define one goal in each of the following categories: health, relationship, and career. Commit to realizing one goal from each category in the next four to six months.

3. Weeks three and four: Create an action plan you are willing to follow to achieve your goals. Write down some power thoughts and images that will support you on your way. Commit to doing something every day that will move you closer to your goal(s).

4. Weeks one to four: Each week, select a difficult situation and consider how you can use it to be more in control and more effective. Define a preparation program that will help you achieve your goal. Follow your preparation program.

5. Weeks two, three, and four: Consider what is challenging, distracting, and stressing you. Use these challenges to intensify your focus and mental toughness.

6. Weeks three and four: Every morning on awakening, spend a moment of relaxed breathing, creating an empowering feeling for the day and a positive self-thought to go with it. Half a dozen times a day, take a breath and recreate that thought and feeling. Affirm: "I am positive and powerful. I am mentally tough. I love a challenge."

CHAPTER TWELVE

INDIVIDUAL DIFFERENCES

"Pressure creates tension and when you're tense you want to get the task over as fast as possible. The more you hurry in golf the worse you probably will play, which leads to even heavier pressure and greater tension. To avoid this vicious circle I'll take a few deep breaths and quickly review why I'm doing what I'm doing."
Jack Nicklaus, PGA Champion

"The pressure makes me more intent on each shot. Pressure on the last few holes makes me play better."
Nancy Lopez, PGA Champion

We're all different. Everyone is unique and special. Most people prefer to minimize pressure for optimal performance. Some, however, seem to thrive on pressure and seek out challenging situations that pump them up. It is very important to discover what works for you.

A few facts of life:

• In our high-pressure, high-stress society, almost everyone can benefit from bringing more ease to their process and improving their ability to relax and reduce stress.

- The most common response to pressure is to contract and tighten up.
- A simple, effective antidote to performance dis-ease, whether it's in a ball game, a conference, a concert, or an exam is to *release... breathe... refocus.* On the other hand, I find that a minority of my clients perform better by increasing (as opposed to decreasing) their level of emotional intensity or arousal. Within limits, their preferred response to pressure is to "pump themselves up."

Tennis, anyone? Tennis was the first sport I worked with, and it presents unique challenges. At the elite level, a match can be two hours of intense competition demanding speed, power, focus and finesse. And it's maximum exposure. You're out there on the court alone. Tennis can be a couple of hours of confrontation with no place to hide, and no one but yourself to blame for a disappointing performance.

Jim P., the Mississippi State University tennis coach, came to see me. He was a former professional tennis player, an ex-army officer, and a graduate of several "mind control" courses. He had great respect for the psychological side of the game and asked if I would do some mental training with the team. We began with breathing and release techniques to develop more emotional control. Then we worked on some "winning programming" that involved combining imaging and good playing mechanics with positive affirmations and power feelings.

One thing I did with the team was to develop a pre-competition routine. Before each match the players would lie down for five to ten minutes with their eyes closed and their racquets in hand. After relaxing and breathing for a few moments, they would mentally run through every aspect of their game and imagine themselves playing well, with speed, balance, power, and accuracy, making all their shots. Most of the players enjoyed the process and found it set them up well.

However, two of the eight team members weren't comfortable with the routine. They said sitting quietly and visualizing before a match made them nervous. Instead of spending a few minutes being quiet and calming down, they wanted to do something energizing to pump themselves up. So we designed a stimulating reaction drill, like shadow boxing that got them moving, and I encouraged them to listen to hard-driving music before a game. I also developed a self-talk program for the players. For most of the team the affirmations were positive, calming, reassuring, and confidence-building. The self-talk created for the two players who wanted more stimulation was very upbeat and challenging. Essentially, it was designed to increase their arousal levels and elicit feelings that would give them an edge and help them to perform.

A few years later, I was working with the Los Angeles Kings of the National Hockey League. In the course of my work I made CDs for several of the players. Confidence-building affirmations and high-performance images were repeated in a supportive, re-assuring voice. The affirmations and images were based on input provided by the players. Again, most of the players enjoyed the CDs and said that listening helped them to feel calmer, centered, focused, and prepared. However, one player approached me after practice one day and said,, "Doc, I've listened to the CD you gave us a few times and I've got to be honest with you. Before a game, I play better if someone yells at me and really gives me shit. It may be strange but that's what helps me to get going." We changed the intensity and the tone of his message accordingly.

There's an old Chinese maxim: one way to reduce fear is to introduce anger. There's no doubt it works in manipulating short-term behavior. The military have used this tactic to move soldiers beyond their fear for centuries. It's also been a standard in sport and business. It used to be that a good kick in the rear (verbally or physically) was one of the principal ways to "motivate." However, times are changing. Coaching (both sport and corporate) is becoming more of a science. The idea that more push often doesn't translate into consistent high-level performance is out there and spreading. In North America the practice of coaching and managing by intimidation seems to be fading about as fast as executive and player salaries are escalating.

Coaching

In both sport and business, leaders are becoming increasingly aware of the benefits of being composed and reassuring when dealing with people under pressure. In baseball, the goal of the pitching coach when addressing a pitcher in a jam is to help him stay positively focused and prevent him from becoming overly tense or anxious. Coaches know that the latter often translates into over-throwing and a loss of accuracy. In sales, managers are learning that the anxieties generated by a slump or a slow start to a campaign can translate into over-selling and a loss of effectiveness. The sales manager, like the pitching coach, can often be more effective facilitating performance by being reassuring and projecting confidence than by simply demanding more.

A coaching formula I often recommend for a baseball manager is this: First, take a breath (or two) to calm yourself. Next, assess the situation. If the decision is to leave the pitcher in the game, it can be helpful if the manager appears confident, reassuring, and projects a positive expectation. The manager or coach should also address specific positives with the pitcher (e.g., what can and will he thrown to get the next batters out).

But sometimes the old style prevails, with good effect. One of the premier relief pitchers in the National League was one of those rare characters who was much more responsive to in-your-face confrontation than to reassurance. In the minor leagues, his manager once confided, "I don't know what to do with this guy. Sometimes he's wild and out of control. But when I try to calm him down, reassure him, he becomes more angry and upset." The answer later came from another pitching coach in the organization who was remarkably successful with the young pitcher. When I asked that coach what he did that was so helpful to the young hurler, he replied, "I challenged him. I told him to cut the nonsense and start throwing strikes, or I'd beat the daylights out of him."

Everyone has an optimal performance range. That's the level of emotional intensity at which he or she performs best. For most people it's just past the mid-point, in the range of a mid to moderate level of emotional arousal (at 6 in the graph below). For some, the optimal level of emotional arousal can be a *little* higher. Generally speaking, if you are either too subdued (low arousal, 2–3 in the graph) or too pumped up (high arousal, 8–9 in the graph) performance drops off.   ***

Figure 12.1 Optimal Performance Range

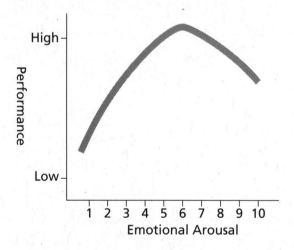

I coach clients to learn what number or level of emotional arousal works best for them. As they prepare to perform, I suggest they assess at what level/number they are. And then (if necessary) use tension-release, breathing, and self-talk to make an adjustment (from too high or too low) to their optimal level.

Commission sales people are under a great deal of pressure to perform. During the six months I "coached" an insurance sales team, I repeatedly explored with the sales manager what helped his team deal most effectively with the pressure of a slow week. For the most part, he advocated being supportive and focusing them on the positives. He acknowledged individual differences of the people on his team and different ways of dealing with them. He was more apt to reassure the sensitive, reserved sales people and challenge some of the more extroverted team members. He cited the example of an excellent saleswoman who became nervous and depressed whenever her numbers dropped. "I remind her to take a breath, then I reassure her that she's a star, and that she can best do the job by going back to the basics." (In insurance sales, that means getting on the phone, making appointments, meeting people, listening to their needs, explaining the benefits, signing the contract, and getting referrals.) He said, "Actually, that's pretty much the approach I take with most of my team."

In sales and in baseball, I think the single most important thing a "coach" can do for an aspiring, young professional is to build self-esteem. Too often the tendency is simply to push more technique at them and demand more. One of the most effective ways to build esteem is to give people a sense of being in control. I do it by teaching them how to regulate emotion, change the channel, and introduce power thoughts and high-performance images, and by repeatedly reminding them that they control the switch.

The best way to coach or manage people varies somewhat according to the people involved and what they do. Different sports and different business functions require different coaching emphases and styles. In baseball and sales it's the *I* or *individual* that is paramount. And it's the *I* or ego that must be stimulated and nurtured to build the performer's confidence and self-esteem. I told the sales manager about the relief pitcher (mentioned earlier) who responded to threats and intimidation and asked him if it was his experience that his salespeople responded better to confrontation than to reassurance. "Oh, there are some I have to poke a little," he replied. "Actually, I used to do more of that barnyard motivation when I first started. You know, take out the verbal cattle prod and give people a jolt to keep them moving forward. Truth is, it moves some people for a short time but it creates resentment. Besides, it's not the way to build a professional sales team. There are very few people in this business who can sustain a high level of performance with threats, intimidation, fear, and abuse. And once you start prodding people you often have to keep prodding to get results. And, even if it did work, I wouldn't want to have to operate like that all the time. It's not the way to build a professional sales team. Most of my team are stimulated by a challenge or a campaign."

These issues are not limited to selling insurance or throwing a baseball. Over-arousal can be limiting in any performance area. Randy was an aspiring member of an improvisational comedy troupe. He was a pleasant young man who put a lot of pressure on himself to make it. Like most performers, when he stepped into the spotlight and center stage, Randy's arousal levels went up. When he tried out new material, his levels went way up, and Randy simply forgot to "use" the people he was playing with. It's the same barrel vision that often limits a distraught or inexperienced quarterback under pressure. For the quarterback, it compresses time and limits his perspective and his perceived options. He feels like the three seconds he has to release the ball is less than two seconds. Pressure-induced barrel vision did the same to Randy. Not surprisingly, it reduced his creativity and effectiveness... and the effectiveness of the whole group of players.

The techniques most helpful to Randy were similar to those we've been describing throughout *Performing Under Pressure*. That is, before a performance Randy took a few minutes to *relax and breathe*, used some *power thinking* to remind himself to be the bright, brave, creative, and entertaining person he is; then he *mentally rehearsed* playing with the other three people on stage in an easy, humorous, creative manner, and recalled and imagined nights of performing very well. On stage, *during* the performance, Randy was encouraged to *breathe*, and *play* loose and easy with his co-actors.

Vive La Différence

Why is it that some people perform better when they relax and calm down, while others need to feel "pumped up" or stimulated to perform at their best? And why do some people thrive on high-pressure jobs (police officer, air traffic controller, emergency room physician, TV news director, hockey goalie, or relief pitcher), while others go into emotional overload at the thought of a high-pressure occupation? There are a number of factors that can account for the different ways people react to pressure.

Are you an introvert or extrovert? One of the differentiating features of personality that accounts for the different ways people handle pressure and stress is introversion and extroversion. In general, introverts tend to be more sensitive and affected by pressure. They overload more easily than extroverts. Extroverts tend to be more stimulus-seeking and may require a higher level of arousal to be at their best. This relationship is depicted in the figure below.

Figure 12.2: Handling Pressure/Optimal Performance Introverts and Extroverts

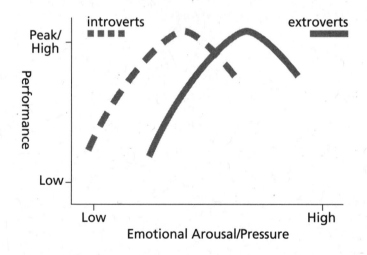

Introverts react poorly to stimulus increases and levels of stimulation or pressure that extroverts might enjoy. They become anxious and tense up; their performance decreases. Introverts

tend to perform better if they learn ways to lower their emotional arousal and stay calm before a contest. Having a clearly defined pre-performance routine helps them manage emotion. It reduces unnecessary last-minute surprises and limits rushing, both of which can be emotionally arousing and anxiety-producing. Introverts prefer for things to occur on time; they take pride and invest time and energy in seeing that all their performance requirements are in order.

While this is useful behavior, a possible downside is that they sometimes become preoccupied with the minor details and the ritual of preparation, and can upset themselves with small deviations in their pre-performance routine. To allay any potential anxiety, it can be useful to remind and encourage the more sensitive and introverted performers to relax. Introverts can benefit from being reassured that they are capable, well-prepared, and that they can deal with any minor alteration in routine or schedule that may present itself. A pre-performance or pre-game breathing session, some positive self-talk, and mental rehearsal are all useful mental skills for more sensitive or introverted performers.

Extroverts, like the relief pitcher mentioned earlier, may need more stimulation and a challenge to get into their optimal arousal zone. They may have difficulty organizing well in advance and often wait until the last minute to really get going. This can lead to some last-minute confusion regarding scheduling their time. It's advisable to encourage extroverts to develop a pre-performance routine that is organizing and helps them to be ready to perform.

Extroverts tend to be social and outgoing; they enjoy interacting with people around them before a game or event, sometimes even challenging them. Introverts are more apt to prepare quietly. They often warm up by themselves. Joking around can be a disturbing pre-event distraction for them before a game. I've observed aggressive extroverts use stimulation and confrontation to get themselves and their associates or teammates "up" before and during a competition. For some people a direct, in-your-face challenge can spark them to perform well. For others, it has the opposite effect.

Most people fall somewhere between the extremes of introversion and extroversion. Understanding who you are and what style works best for you can be very helpful. One thing you can do to gain insight is to reflect on those times when you performed at your best. Think back and ask yourself what you had done to prepare on those high-performance days.

Most people have some sense of where they fit on the introversion-extroversion continuum. If you want some feedback, one of the best tests available is the Myers Briggs Type Indicator (MBTI)[1] I use the test in my work, both in facilitating elite athletic performance and with corporate and management teams.

There are several other personality features that differentiate people and performance styles. The Myers Briggs looks at four dimensions. One dimension differentiates the more data conscious,

---

1. The Meyers Briggs Type Indicator (MBTI) is available through Consulting Psychologists Press, Palo Alto, CA. For more information see: Isobel Meyers Briggs, Peter B. Meyers, *Understanding Personality Type*.

factual individual (S) from the more intuitive, possibilities-minded (N) type. Another dimension contrasts the analytic, thinking, task-oriented (T) individual, from the more empathetic, feeling-oriented (F) type. And a fourth dimension differentiates people who prefer routines (J) from those who prefer spontaneity and diversity (P).

The Test of Attentional and Interpersonal Style (TAIS)[2] is another personality style inventory, that differentiates the way people focus. The test defines two dimensions of focusing style: broad to narrow focus, and external to internal focus. Healthy people have the capacity to shift to all four focusing styles (broad external, broad internal, narrow external, narrow internal) depending on the task required: For example, a broad external focus would be most appropriate for a point guard, quickly scanning the court as he brings up the ball. A narrow internal focus might be the focusing style employed in doing relaxing imagery. Most people have a preferred focusing style that predisposes them to perceive and react to things differently.

People with different personality and focusing styles tend to deal with pressure differently. Understanding these differences can help an individual, and a manager or coach, make work-related adjustments and decisions that can enhance the capacity to perform under pressure.

Mark was a Rams linebacker, a special teams captain and a super-intense competitor. I was asked to develop a simple

2. Linda V Berens, *The Dynamics of Personality Type*, Temperament Research Institute, Telos Publications, Huntington Beach, CA. For more information see The Attention and Interpersonal Style Inventory (TAIS) http://www.rembisz/com/tais3.html.

program for him that he could use in the game to deal with a specific performance pressure issue. Mark would get so intense in games that he would develop performance-limiting cramps. In terms of personality style mentioned above, he was a more extroverted, feeling-oriented, (E,F,P) performer with a broad external focus. The first season we worked together on conscious breathing, release techniques and mental rehearsal. The next year he became a starter and wanted something to keep him from getting too intense. He specifically wanted to have more control of his emotions, to focus more clearly on the task requirements, to make the right reads, and to be able to react at his best, play after play.

Based on his personality style and the task at hand, we developed a special program for him. Between every play, Mark would think, "A, B, C, D, E, F, G, H." A, B, C was A = always, B = breathe, and C = get calm. As soon as the play was over, Mark would think ABC, take a few breaths and calm down. Then, a little more at ease (and possessing the judgment that calmness can bring) he'd switch his focus externally to the task at hand and think D, E, F, G, H. The D meant down and distance (e.g., second and two, or third and eight). The E meant evaluate (Mark would review the probabilities of what the opposition was likely to do in that situation). The F referred to formation (e.g., two wide receivers right, or two tight ends in, wide receiver left). Each formation cued Mark to specific responsibilities. Then Mark would think G, for guard. He'd read the guard for pass and run probabilities. Lastly

Mark would think H for hit, which meant intensify emotion and be ready for war.

Mark was an emotional performer with a broad focus. The program matched his personality and focusing needs and worked extremely well. It was simple enough to remember even under the intense emotion of the game, and it gave Mark the ability to regulate his feelings and focus on the key externals to be effective. Mark had an excellent season that year. For the first 15 games of the season he led the team in tackles.

Take Stock

Sit down and reflect on two or three times in the recent past when you performed very well. Recall your preparation for the event and the buildup to it. Recall how you felt and what you did immediately prior to competition. Individual differences are real. There are some marked differences on what feels "right" and what facilitates different individuals.

Whether you are a performer/player, coach, or manager, to optimize your ability to perform under pressure, it's important to understand and respect individual differences, to know who you are, and put that knowledge to good use.

TRAINING NOTES

Know Thyself

Monitor your feelings.

Develop a pre-performance behavior pattern that feels good and works for you. One way to do that is to recall two or three times when you performed at your best. Then recall two or three times when your performance was disappointing. In both cases write down as much as you can recall about how you felt on those days.

Were you confident? Were you clear? Were you able to focus or concentrate? Were you calm, pumped up, or nervous? (Some athletes monitor their pulse rate to determine if they are in their optimal performance range. If their heart rate is faster than what they've determined is their pre-competition ideal, or if they feel too excited, they calm themselves down. On the other hand, if their heart rate is too low, or if they feel under-aroused, they pump themselves up.)

Did you feel ready to perform or unprepared? Were you positive or worried? What were you thinking about? Were you on time, early, or late?

Do some self-evaluation as to your personality style.

- Are you more introverted or extroverted?
- Are you more task-oriented or more people oriented?

- Do you have a broad focus or are you more of a detail person?
- Do you prefer set routines or spontaneity and diversity?
- Are you more internal or external in your focus?

There is no right or wrong, but understanding your style can help you make better career and life choices and adjustments.

- Define or develop a pre-performance pattern that helps you to be at your best.
- From here on, begin to observe your behavior when you're about to perform. Remember, you can't always control the external circumstances surrounding your performance; however, when it comes to how you feel, and think, it's your TV. You control the switch.

CHAPTER THIRTEEN

A HIGH-PERFORMANCE LIFESTYLE

In writing *Performing Under Pressure* I wanted to communicate the simplest components that would have the greatest effect on enhancing the ability to perform under pressure. What I came up with was a combination of positive programming and the release, breathe, refocus formula. It's basic. However, there are other factors that are also extremely important in nurturing your ability to perform under pressure. One of them is lifestyle. For several years, whenever I spoke to business groups across North America I would ask the audience two questions. Question One: which factors have most contributed to your growth and success?

The three most frequent responses to the first question were a positive attitude; hard work; and being surrounded by positive, talented, hardworking people.

The second question was "What, if anything, could limit your continued growth and success?" The overwhelming response was a factor that is rarely given any training time or attention in performance-enhancement seminars: health.

People know that if they're sick (or dead!) they won't perform very well. And they're becoming more conscious of some of the basic ingredients that nurture health and consistent high-level performance. The list includes diet, exercise, recreation, relaxation, relationships, and a healthy perspective.

We don't live in a vacuum. We live in a biochemical, psychophysical, socioeconomic life space. Our ability to think clearly, focus, manage stress, and excel under pressure is directly affected by how we live in this space. What you eat, your exercise, recreation, rest, and social patterns all have a profound effect on how you express yourself in the game of life.

Pay attention to your diet.

Eat to be a consistent winner in regard to both performance and well-being. The nervous system operates on biochemical impulses. What you eat affects your stress tolerance, the quality of your programming, and your ability to change channels. When I worked in the NFL, I noticed the players' parking area was loaded with high-priced cars. Occasionally, when I observed a player eating junk food for breakfast, I would ask him what he was driving. When he named some high-performance automobile I would say, "You wouldn't put poor quality fuel in your car and expect it to perform well. Why not respect yourself the same way?"

The standard North American diet is high in fat, high in protein, and high in sugar and chemicals. While a cheeseburger, fries, and a cola may appeal to some people's taste buds and support short-term "start-stop" energy, in the long run it's stressful to the organism. Over time, it reduces health and performance and in-creases our vulnerability to stress and dis-ease.

Many experts recommend a diet rich in complex carbohydrates with an abundance of unrefined grains, vegetables and fruits, and a moderate intake of fat and protein.[1]

Your diet should also be relatively free from refined sugars. Cookies, candy, cake, and colas can be an unhealthy habit and an addictive one. They appeal entirely to our sense of taste. Artificial sweetners aren't any better. Most of them have been shown to have an unhealthy side effects. Refined sugars can be unbalancing and stressful. If you want something sweet, eat fruit.

Your diet should be *moderate in protein*. Most North Americans could cut their protein intake by a third. Look for alternatives to animal protein. I used to say to people, "You don't need to eat meat everyday." Now I say (and there's research to support this), "It can be a health risk to be eating meat everyday."

Your diet needs to be *relatively free from refined sugars*. Cookies, candy, cakes, and colas can be an unhealthy habit and an addictive one. They appeal entirely to our sense of taste. Artificial sweet-eners aren't any better. (Most of them have been shown to have significant unhealthy side effects.) Simple sugars are the fuel of the nervous system. Refined sugars can be unbalancing and stressful. If you want something sweet, eat fruit.

---

1. Over 30 years ago a British Medical Journal editorial stated, "Few nutritionists now dis-pute that Western man (and woman) eat too much meat, too much animal fat and dairy products, too much refined carbohydrate and too little dietary fibre. Epidemiological studies of hear disease suggest that some at least of the deaths in middle age from myo-cardial infarction could be cut by a move towards a more prudent diet--which means more cereal grains and less meat. " British Medical Journal 2 (1977b): 0-81.

Your diet should be *sensible*. Get into the habit of choosing simple preparations of wholesome foods as opposed to foods that are highly processed and loaded with chemical additives. And avoid overeating.

Additionally, *avoid "drugs."* I can't think of a faster way to lose control of the mental switch than by doing drugs. Yet the use of drugs, prescription or otherwise, to both stimulate and to reduce stress and "dis-ease" is epidemic in our culture. There are no silver bullets. If you're looking for enhanced or altered states, develop your ability to release, breathe, and focus. Remember, the "response-ability" is yours. Looking to drugs to support the effect you want will ultimately result in dependency, a loss of power, and *more* stress.

Coffee and alcohol are popular drugs. Coffee is a stimulant, and alcohol a central nervous system depressant. Don't be in the habit of relying on coffee for a lift and alcohol to mellow you out. Be moderate in their use.

It seems there is also an epidemic of taking drugs to enhance performance. This is particularly evident in baseball. A number of the game's top players have tested positive to using performance-enhancing drugs. This trend is not limited to baseball. What's particularly disturbing about this drug-aided push to perform is that people are willing to risk health and well-being for a result. Back in the mid-eighties, Dr. Robert Goldman asked 198 world-class athletes, "Would you take a pill that would guarantee you a gold medal even if they knew it would kill you in five years?"—and

103 of the 198 said they would.[2] Things haven't improved. More people than ever are looking for the silver bullet to provide them with a performance boost and are willing to do self-destructive things to get that competitive edge. There's an alternative. Power thinking and imagery, conscious breathing, a winning attitude, and a healthy lifestyle will enhance both performance and quality of life, and do it without any deleterious side effects.

Exercise intelligently.

An excellent way to increase your resistance to pressure and stress is to exercise and be in good physical shape. And one of the best ways to get into shape is to be on the move. People are made to move. Dynamic exercise, movement, and action all stimulate energy flow. They are a balance to too much "sitting and thinking" at a computer or watching TV. Walking, jogging, cycling, dancing, swimming are all fine. Action games like racket ball and tennis are also fine, provided you don't take them so seriously that they become an additional source of stress.

Most experts recommend a minimum of four 20-minute periods of accelerated movement each week. Along with aerobic movement, some stretching and strengthening exercises are also advisable. Avoid making your exercise sessions too violent, especially if you haven't been working out regularly. Overdoing it can result in more stress and strain then it prevents. I have seen far

2. Dr. Robert Goldman, *Death in the Locker Room: Steroids & Sports*, Icarus Press, 1984.

too many people who have injured themselves by a weekend of extreme exercise as well as those with sore legs and backs from jogging excessively on hard pavement. But the data is in, and the results are crystal clear; exercising *intelligently and regularly* will enhance your ability to handle pressure and stress.

Experience quality recreation.

To re-create means to re-new. Think of things that you do that renew you, that *give* you energy. They may include sport, exercise, the arts (playing music, painting, dancing, cooking,) reading, listening to music, being with people (conversing, being close) or being quiet (e.g., meditating). You are response-able to create healthy recreational habits. Regularly do things that are energizing, balancing, and that you *enjoy*. Enjoyment adds life and energy to the process.

TV is North America's most common form of entertainment. However, it's not true recreation. There are very few people, if any, who get up after watching three or four hours of television and say, "I feel great." For most people TV is more of a diversion or escape from the stresses and pressures they are experiencing. Cultivate recreational patterns that renew you.

Re-lax.

The word "relax" means to regain a natural feeling of looseness and ease. As such, relaxation is the perfect balance to tension and dis-ease. It's a mind-body process that promotes health, healing, and longevity. Relaxation addresses all systems. It improves respiratory efficiency. It lowers heart rate and blood pressure. It reduces muscle tension. And it balances the activity of the left and right cerebral hemispheres of the brain.

In this book, I have described in some detail how to relax your breathing as well as different muscle groups in the body, and how to tune out worry and negative thoughts that increase tension and stress. These are not separate elements. They all blend together. As you tune into your breathing, allow your body to relax. As your body relaxes, it becomes easier to breathe. As you breathe more easily, your mind becomes more centered and calm. As the mind calms, the body relaxes and thinking becomes clearer and more positive.

Relaxation is one of the keys to a high-performance lifestyle. Incorporate your knowledge and experience of relaxation into both your performance challenges and your daily life. Experience it in its most simple instantaneous form as a 10-second timeout (breathe, release, refocus), or as 20 connected breaths. Take a five-minute "power break" a couple of times during the day. Have a 15-minute "relaxation time out" at a low-energy point in your day. The thing to remember is that relaxing can be energizing, recharging, balancing, and *it feels good*. Allow yourself to relax. You deserve to feel good. And you control the switch.

Develop empowering relationships.

The second most frequent response to the question "What could limit your continued growth and success?" was "negativity."

Working, living, and performing with negative people is a tremendous drain on anyone's personal energy. Like our health, the social context in which we live and perform can be nurturing or limiting. Whenever possible, create relationships that are supportive, positive, and that empower you. Seek out winners—positive people who look to the potential and the possibility that lies within us all.

If possible, avoid people who are negative, critical, and destructive. If your reality is to live and work with negative, destructive people, *use* the experience as an opportunity to develop more psycho-physical control, repeatedly release and breathe, and stay tuned into the love, power, and possibility channel. Take from their message what is useful, be willing to communicate, and work at being less attached to their approval.

You can't always control the circumstances in your life, but you are response-able to control your reactions to them. Part of learning how to succeed in the face of a meaningful challenge is maintaining that kind of healthy perspective. If there's a single concluding thought, it is that winners love and enjoy the challenge, and the opportunity to excel, as well as the pressure that goes with it.

Whatever your endeavor, I encourage you to acknowledge your remarkable self.

Empower yourself with breath and thought.

Embrace the challenges you face, and go for the gold with a smile.

ABOUT THE AUTHOR

Dr. Saul L. Miller is one of North America's leading performance and sport psychologists. He is a consultant, counselor, speaker, artist, and author of eight books, including *Hockey Tough* and *Why Teams Win: 9 Keys to Success in Business, Sport, and Beyond*. Dr. Miller consults with sport teams, corporations, and health organizations across North America. The focus of his work is enhancing performance, team building, and helping people achieve success while dealing effectively with pressure, stress, and change.

In sport, he has worked with the New York Mets, Seattle Mariners, Los Angeles Dodgers, Rams, Clippers, and Kings, Florida Panthers, St. Louis Blues, Vancouver Canucks, and Nashville Predators, plus PGA Tour golfers and Olympians from the USA, Canada, and Europe in over a dozen different sports.

In business his clients come from management, manufacturing, and sales and service. He has consulted with financial services, technology, insurance, the building and service industries, and health care. For six years Dr. Miller ran a successful health care facility treating pain and disability and helping people get back to living a healthy, productive life.

There is no one in North America with more "hands on" experience facilitating success and well-being. Dr. Miller's clients have increased sales volumes 100 percent, improved management "coaching" effectiveness, set records, won championships and gold medals, and improved their health and well-being.

He is a graduate of McGill University and the Institute of Psychiatry, University of London (Ph.D. Clinical Psychology). His work reflects his study of Eastern disciplines, Western psychological thinking, and over 25 years of front line experience consulting with some of the world's top performers.

BIBLIOGRAPHY

Bartlett's Familiar Quotations, 16th edition

Bats by Davey Johnson and Peter Golenbock, G.P. Putnam & Sons, NY, 1986

Body Learning, An Introduction to the Alexander Technique, by Michael Gelb, Henry
Holt & Co., NY 1996.

Death in the Locker Room, by B. Goldman, South Bend, IN: Icarus Press, 1984.

Fitness Without Stress: A Guide to the Alexander Technique, by Robert Rickover, Metamorphosos Press, 1988.

Hockey Tough: Winning the Mental Game, by Dr. Saul L. Miller, Human Kinetics, Champaign, IL, 2003.

Mental Toughness Training For Sports, by James E. Loehr, The Stephen Greene Press, New York, 1986.

One Minute Manager, by Kenneth Blanchard and Spencer Johnson, William Morrow and Company Inc., 1982.

The Alchemist, by Paulo Coelho, Harper Collins, 2006.

The Dynamics of Personality Type, by Linda V Berens, Temperament Research Institute,
Telos Publications, Huntington Beach, CA.

The Edge, by Ferguson, Howard (ed.) Getting The Edge Co., Cleveland, Ohio, 1983.

The Inner Game of Tennis, by W. Timothy Gallwey, Random House, May, 1974.

Understanding Personality Type, by Isobel Meyers Briggs, Peter B. Meyers.

Why Teams Win: 9 Keys to Success in Business, Sport, and Beyond, by Dr. Saul L.
Miller, John Wiley & Sons, Toronto, Canada, 2009.

Zen Flesh, Zen Bones, by Paul Reps, Charles. E. Tuttle Inc. Publishers, 1957.

INDEX

bull image, 64
bullwhip image, 64–65
business, and sport, 67

C

calming down, 167–168
Cam, 132–133
capability, 199–200
Carole, 99–100
Cathy, 180–181
cat image, 64
"cat's feet," 58, 103, 149
cellist, 190–191
center, balance, refocus, 112
cerebral hemispheres, 108
challenges (defining and setting), 80
challenging thoughts, 31
changing channels, 77
changing our minds, 59
chest, 98–99
chi, 105
choking, 99–100
clarity
    and breathing, 142, 144
    and motivation, 176, 177
    and motivational pressure, 23
Cliff, 192–193
coaching, 210–215
coaching formula, 211
Coelho, Paulo, 137
coffee, 228
cold calling, 124
commitment, 175, 179–185
confidence, 156, 175, 185–192
conscious brain, 7
conscious breathing, 105
consumer society, 123
continuity of breath, 131–146
contractive reactions, 152
contractive reflex, 88, 91, 100
control, 21
"control of the switch," 93

corporate goal-setting conference, 39–41
creating change, 63
creative pressure, 15
Curt, 166
cycling team, 81–85

D

Dan, 32–35
data conscious factual individual, 218–219
Dave, 158–159
David, 161
Dawn, 161
daydreaming (mental rehearsal), 53
Deborah, 199
defensive contraction reflex, 95
defining
    goal, 23, 63
    and mental rehearsal, 53
    self, 25–27
deserving, 175, 192–194
desire, 8, 12, 23
diet, 226–229
differences, 207–223
difficulty, 80–81, 83
dis-ease (pressure), 7, 8, 41
divers, 20, 195–197
Dodgers pitcher, 107–109, 159–160
the Doing, 19
doing into being, 28–29
dolphin image, 64
Don, 114–116
Doug, 64, 199
downhill racers, 147–148
drugs, 228–229
dynamic exercise, 229

E

ease up, pull down, 96
Edmonton Oilers, 41
ego, 214
Einstein, Albert, 52, 70